Georgia Snapshots

Georgia Snapshots

Glances at the Past

James E. Kloeppel

Adele Enterprises
Union City, Georgia

Published by: Adele Enterprises
            PO Box 553
            Union City, GA 30291-0553

Manufactured in the United States of America

Publisher's Cataloging-in-Publication Data

Kloeppel, James E.
    Georgia snapshots : glances at the past / James E. Kloeppel.
        p. cm.
    Includes index.
    ISBN 0-9640374-0-8
    1. Georgia — Guidebooks — History. I. Title
F284.3.K56 1994
917.58

Library of Congress Catalog Card Number: 94-70129

Contents

Chapter 5: Early Industry and Trade

Chapter 6: The Best Dam Sites in Georgia

Chapter 7: Georgia Potpourri

Chapter 8: There's No Place Like Home

Chapter 9: In Defense of the Land

Chapter 10: Lest We Forget

Preface

From the North Georgia mountains to the rolling Piedmont to the colonial coast, Georgia is a land rich in history. Covered bridges, gristmills, lighthouses, forts, battlefields, and the homes of the rich and famous all speak vividly of the past. *Georgia Snapshots* is a book about those special places, an illustrative guide to some of the very best historic sites in this peach of a state.

To create *Georgia Snapshots*, over 200 sites were researched and visited, of which the best 64 were chosen. Site selection criteria included such factors as historical significance, aesthetics, human interest, and accessibility. If I could not honestly recommend a particular site to a friend, it was not included in this book.

Each site is represented by a photographic "snapshot" showing the site as it appears today, and by a written "snapshot" encapsulating the site's history. Addresses, directions, visiting hours, admission fees, and telephone numbers are listed in the appendix. As visiting hours and admission fees are subject to change, it is a good idea to call ahead.

I would like to thank the many individuals who suggested potential sites for this book, and the many librarians and historians who provided helpful tidbits of information. Sincere appreciation goes to my friend and colleague, Mark Hodges, who reviewed the manuscript and offered suggestions for its improvement. Special thanks go to Dr. James Brittain, professor of history, technology, and society at the Georgia Institute of Technology, for his advice and encouragement; and to my wife, Darlene, for her enduring support. Special thanks also go to my children, Christopher, Betty, Jonathan, and Thomas, for accompanying me on the many field trips and for making this project so much fun.

If you have a favorite site which you feel should be included in a future edition of *Georgia Snapshots*, please let me know. A form has been included in the back of this book for your convenience.

Best wishes, and may your future be even brighter than your past!

Chapter 1:

Native Americans and Ancient Cultures

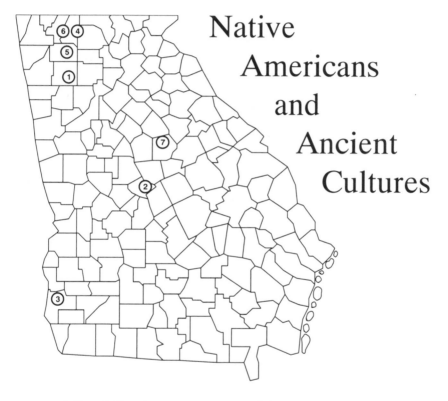

1 Etowah Mounds
2 Ocmulgee National Monument
3 Kolomoki Mounds
4 Fort Mountain

5 New Echota
6 Vann House
7 Rock Eagle Effigy Mound

Etowah Mounds

Rising mysteriously above the flat floodplain of the Etowah
River near Cartersville in Northwest Georgia, the Etowah Indian
Mounds tell of a time and culture long past. The people who once
inhabited the Etowah site formed part of a broad, well-developed
Mississippian culture that stretched from the Atlantic Ocean west
to the Mississippi River Valley and north to Ohio. Huge mounds,
constructed from hundreds of thousands of basket loads of dirt,
were central to the Indians' religious beliefs and social customs.

The great temple mound, one of three earthen structures on the
Etowah site, rises 63 feet toward the heavens and is the largest of
the "American Pyramids" in Georgia. This awesome mound
appears today much as it did hundreds of years ago, seemingly

2

untouched by the long fingers of time. On its summit stood a wooden temple where the chief priest presided over religious and cultural ceremonies. The flat land surrounding the mounds was peppered with hundreds of simple, rectangular-shaped thatched huts.

Like many other Mississippian sites, the town was fortified against attack from marauding bands of hostile Indians. A portion of the nearby Etowah River was diverted into a wide moat excavated around the sprawling 52-acre village. A sturdy palisade of upright posts and intertwined limbs erected around the village perimeter offered additional protection.

Using spears and arrows, the Etowah Indians hunted deer, bear, beaver, opossum, squirrel, and rabbit. The larger animals not only provided flesh for food, but supplied skin for clothing, hooves for rattles, and bones for tools. The Indians also caught catfish, gar, and drum using simple but effective fish traps built of rocks and woven baskets.

Although traditional hunting and gathering remained important, the Etowah Indians increasingly relied on agriculture, tilling the fertile soil with primitive digging sticks and hoes fashioned from chipped flint or animal bone. They supplemented their domestic crops of corn, beans, and squash with such natural edibles as hickory nuts, walnuts, blackberries, and persimmon.

Unlike the great temple mound, two smaller mounds at Etowah were erected for the sole purpose of burying the dead. These mounds were periodically enlarged, layer by layer. Over 350 burials took place in the smaller of the two mounds.

The Mississippian Indians developed elaborate mortuary customs, frequently burying pottery, jewelry, and other fancy grave goods with the deceased. At Etowah, two marble statues, representing a man and a woman, were found interred together near the bottom of the smaller burial mound. These and thousands of other artifacts continue to provide valuable insight into the lives and beliefs of these now vanished mound builders.

Ocmulgee National Monument

Nearly 11 centuries ago, a band of migrants slowly began moving east from the Mississippi River Valley. Upon encountering the verdant Macon Plateau, they went no further. There, on a beautiful bluff beside the Ocmulgee River, they built an elaborate town of thatched huts and earthen mounds. Skillful farmers, they planted extensive crops of beans, corn, and squash in fields along the fertile river bottoms.

Today, these historic people are called the Mississippian Indians, and their now-abandoned site has become the Ocmulgee National Monument. The intricate religious beliefs and social customs developed by these primitive Americans are still being unraveled as park personnel continue to peer into the past.

The Great Temple Mound, rising 50 feet above the Macon Plateau, dominates the Ocmulgee site. This huge, flat-topped mound, its massive base covering more than an acre and a half, was apparently used by the chief priest during religious ceremonies. The significance of a much smaller adjacent mound, however, has thus far been lost to history.

Standing alone on the west side of town, the pyramidal Funeral Mound was reserved for interring important village leaders. The dead were prepared for burial in a rectangular-shaped mortuary building perched atop the mound. More than 100 burials have been unearthed here. Unfortunately, railroad construction in the 1870s destroyed much of the mound.

Another structure central to the Mississippian culture stood on the north side of town. Built of sturdy pine logs and covered with dirt, this circular edifice served as a ceremonial meeting place for the town elders. Nearly 42 feet in diameter, the earth-lodge contained a large central firepit, a raised clay platform shaped like a bird, and a low clay bench running along the inner wall. The present structure has been reconstructed based on archeological evidence.

Sometime around 1100 AD, the Mississippian age at Macon drew suddenly to a close. Of the more than 1000 individuals who occupied Ocmulgee at its peak, all have disappeared without a trace. Whether they died from an epidemic, became restless and moved elsewhere, or were assimilated into some other culture may never be known. But the legacy they left behind lives on in the mysterious mounds of Macon.

Kolomoki Mounds

More than 700 years ago, Kolomoki grew in great tribal significance to the Woodland Indians who occupied what would later become Southwestern Georgia. Kolomoki literally rose from the ground as its ancient inhabitants toiled at their incredible task, creating huge mounds of earth upon which they would practice their religion and bury their dead. Long before European explorers trekked across the continent, Kolomoki had become a major population and ceremonial center in North America. As many as 3,000 inhabitants may have lived and worshipped at the site during its glorious peak in the 13th century.

Situated along Kolomoki Creek just a few miles from the Chattahoochee River, this 300-acre prehistoric site includes nine impressive earthen mounds. Eclipsing the others, the Great Temple Mound is by far the largest, formed from an estimated two million basket loads of dirt which demanded the labor of some 1,000 workers. Rising 56 feet above the surrounding plain, the enormous mound covers nearly an acre and a half. From its summit, the chief priest led the riverine agriculturalists in the elaborate religious rituals which governed not only their lives, but their deaths as well.

Immediately in front of the Great Temple Mound was a large open plaza which doubled as playing field and village commons. Half a dozen burial mounds lay scattered about the plaza perimeter. The dead were placed in carefully prepared log-lined graves and covered by a layer of rock and thick mantle of earth. Typical of the Woodland culture, a variety of grave goods accompanied the dead on their final journey. These offerings included beads, conch shells, clay effigies, and pottery vessels which had been symbolically "killed" by knocking holes through the bottoms.

Archaeologists studying the Kolomoki site have also unearthed a number of strange cymbal-shaped ornaments hammered from copper and meteoric iron. The special significance of these ornaments is as yet unknown. Indeed, much concerning the rapid rise and eventual fall of this mysterious race of mound builders remains a puzzle to this day.

Fort Mountain

High atop Fort Mountain, the most prominent peak in the Cohutta Mountain Range of North Georgia, an ancient wall of piled rock stretches to the horizon. The origin of this old stone wall, which weaves across the summit's southern face for 855 feet, is wrapped in mystery and legend. Carefully constructed circular pits, built into the wall at regular intervals, and the ruins of an old gateway add to the riddle of the unknown builders and the purpose of their handiwork.

According to Cherokee Indian legends, the wall was erected by a mysterious race of fair-skinned, yellow-haired people the Cherokees called "Moon Eyes" because of their supposedly keen night vision. Many modern theories, proposed by archaeologists and historians, appear equally fantastic.

One theory, which once received wide support, claims the wall was built by gold-seeking Spanish conquistadors as a fortification against Indian attacks. Another theory credits the wall's construction to a 14th century band of wandering Welsh explorers, again as a defense against hostile Indians. However, many experts doubt that either the conquistadors or the Welsh explorers remained in the Fort Mountain area long enough to build the wall. Possessing vastly superior weapons, it is also questionable whether the intruders would have required such a fortification. Indeed, the wall's low profile and limited length would have afforded but little protection.

More likely, as most experts now believe, the wall was erected for religious or ceremonial purposes by an unknown tribe of sun worshippers nearly 15 centuries ago. Significantly, the wall extends from a cliff on the east side of the summit to another cliff on the west side, thus providing unobstructed views of the rising and setting sun. The complete absence of artifacts in the wall's vicinity also lends support to this theory. Except when offered in ritual burials, ceremonial objects were carefully guarded and taken with the Indians when they moved to a new location.

Whether built for defense, ritual, or worship, the ancient ruins have stimulated the imagination of visitors for hundreds of years. Today, the old stone wall, with its many secrets locked forever in the rocks, is part of Fort Mountain State Park. One of Georgia's finest, the park is located seven miles east of Chatsworth.

New Echota

During the early 19th century, the Cherokee Indian Nation stretched across present-day northern Georgia into western North Carolina, eastern Tennessee, and northeastern Alabama. At the center of this vast sovereign land, in the year 1825, the Cherokees established a new government seat. Named for

Chota, an old beloved town in Tennessee, New Echota soon became the sad focus of a terrible clash between the peoples of two nations.

Perhaps surprisingly, the Cherokee People had become well adapted to the ways of the growing multitudes of white settlers who were threatening their land. They had adopted a republican form of government patterned after the United States, and established an effective legal process for resolving disputes. At New Echota, the Cherokees erected a large legislative hall, a supreme court house, and a print shop for a national newspaper unique among American Indians at that time. Made possible by a syllabary invented by a mixed-blood Cherokee named Sequoyah, the first issue of "Tsalagi Tsulehisanunhi" (the Cherokee Phoenix) rattled off the presses in February of 1828.

Later that same year, Georgia passed an ignoble act annexing the Indian lands which fell within the state's borders. Thus began the Cherokee's futile 10-year struggle to retain their land. In 1835, a small band of Cherokees signed the treaty of New Echota, which effectually exchanged native land in the East for land in the West, far beyond Georgia. Though protested by a majority of the Cherokees, the treaty was ratified by the U.S. Congress the following year. The Cherokees were given two years in which to move.

Reluctant to leave, most remained on their lands until late 1838, when U.S. soldiers rounded them up and hauled them off to what is now eastern Oklahoma. Nearly 4,000 Indians died on the tortuous winter trek, a tragic journey which became known as the Trail of Tears.

When the last of the Cherokees had been driven away, New Echota quickly faded from maps and memory. Today, the partially reconstructed townsite lies just off Interstate 75 near Calhoun.

Vann House

Located on the old Federal Road just west of Chatsworth — deep in the heart of what was once Indian territory — the Vann House stands today in silent tribute to the Cherokee Nation. The house was built for James Vann, a wealthy Cherokee Indian chief who owned a profitable plantation and frontier trading post. The son of a Scottish trader and a Cherokee woman, Vann proved a shrewd and successful businessman. Generous when sober but onerous when he had been drinking, Vann was said to have been "feared by many and loved by few." But Chief Vann is perhaps best remembered for his help in establishing the Moravian Mission at nearby Spring Place in 1801, an act which brought formal education and other lasting benefits to his people.

In 1804, Vann decided to build for himself a magnificent mansion, one which would also serve as a showpiece for the entire Cherokee Nation. Highly skilled Moravian craftsmen, Indian workers, and plantation slaves built the house using materials found locally. Bricks of fine Georgia clay were formed and fired on the site. Lumber was cut and planed in the plantation sawmill; nails, hinges, and other metalwork were fashioned in Vann's own blacksmith shop. The fine, two-story mansion was decorated with beautiful Cherokee hand-carved woodwork painted in four traditional Indian colors: blue represented the sky, green the grass and trees, yellow the harvest fields, and red the Georgia clay.

On March 24, 1805, the Vann family moved into their magnificent new home. Just four years later, however, the 41-year-old chief was fatally shot during a dispute at nearby Buffington's Tavern. Vann's wonderful "Show Place of the Cherokee Nation" passed to his youngest son Joseph.

13

For a quarter of a century Joseph Vann prospered on the plantation, significantly expanding his father's business ventures. In the mid-1830s, however, the Vann family became victims of Georgia's rush for Indian removal. When Vann unknowingly violated a new Georgia law by hiring a white man to work for him as overseer of the plantation, the State quickly seized his property, forcing Vann and his family to flee into Tennessee. Anxious for white settlement, the government divided Vann's vast holdings into 160-acre parcels and distributed them in the land lottery.

Joseph Vann eventually won a meager settlement from the Federal Government in the 1840s. For his fine brick home, trading post, and plantation (with its dozens of cabins, shops, mills, and barns, and its hundreds of acres of fields and orchards), Vann received the paltry sum of $19,605.

Over the years, the Vann House has had a number of owners. Some cared for the property, while many others did not. By 1950, time had taken a heavy toll on the once beautiful structure: the roof had rotted away, floors had collapsed, and windows had been shattered by vandals. In 1952, the Whitfield-Murray Historical Society purchased the house and presented it to the Georgia Historical Commission. The house was restored and opened as a state historic site in 1958.

Rock Eagle
Effigy Mound

More than 50 centuries ago, a mysterious race of early North American builders piled thousands upon thousands of rocks into the shape of an enormous bird. Located in what later became the heart of Georgia, about five miles north of Eatonton, Rock Eagle Effigy Mound still sports a wingspan of over 100 feet. The chunks of rock remain heaped in some places 10 feet high, and range in size from baseballs to boulders. The Eagle's head symbolically faces east, greeting each new sunrise. Believed to be older than the Great Pyramids of Egypt, the effigy no doubt played a significant role in the religious life of the ancient and unknown people who created it.

Chapter 2:

Sentries
by
the
Sea

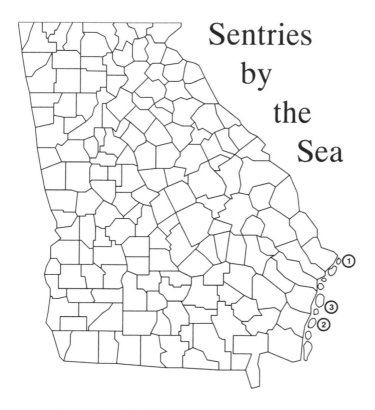

1 Tybee Island Lighthouse
2 St. Simons Lighthouse
3 Sapelo Island Lighthouse

Tybee Island Lighthouse

They have been called sentries by the sea, and their remains litter seacoasts around the world. Of Georgia's 18 original lighthouses, only five remain standing today. The oldest and tallest of these coastal signposts is located on Tybee Island at the mouth of the Savannah River.

The first lighthouse on Tybee was erected in 1736, a scant

three years after General James Oglethorpe established his colony at Savannah. The beacon stood 90 feet tall, and lasted five years before being swept away by a freak summer storm. A new tower, 94 feet high, was completed the following year. But when the sea once again threatened to claim what man had built, a new site much farther inland was selected, and a sturdy, octagonal-shaped structure of brick and wood was begun. Topping out at 100 feet, the new lighthouse was finally finished in 1773.

Nearly 100 years later, when Confederate forces abandoned their weak fortifications on Tybee Island in 1862, soldiers blew up the top third of the lighthouse to prevent its use by the Federal navy. In 1867, the damaged structure was rebuilt. Instead of building from the ground up, workers simply cleared away rubble down to the intact 60-foot level, then began adding new brick.

The finished lighthouse rose an impressive 154 feet; its massive masonry walls, 12 feet thick at the base, tapered to just 18 inches below the cupola at the top. Staffed with a responsible lighthouse keeper, Tybee Island Lighthouse began a new era of standing guard at the dangerous intersection of sea and shore.

Several times a day, the lighthouse keeper climbed the 183 steps leading to the top, hauling up heavy cans of fuel to feed the hungry oil lamp during the night. There were other duties to perform as well, such as meticulously cleaning the glass lamp and reflector assembly, and polishing the brass components.

In 1933, the lighthouse's old oil lamp was replaced with a more powerful and efficient electric light. Fifteen years later, with the death of lighthouse keeper George Jackson, the U.S. Coast Guard fully automated the structure.

Today, the tower's brilliant 1000-watt lamp emits a beacon visible more than 18 miles out to sea. Although open to the public through the courtesy of the Tybee Island Historical Society, the lighthouse remains an active and essential aid to navigation on the Savannah waterway.

St. Simons Lighthouse

St. Simons is the largest, and perhaps the most historically interesting, of Georgia's "Golden Isles." Long before James Edward Oglethorpe first scouted the island for colonial defensive purposes in 1733, native Americans had frequently visited to feast upon oysters and other abundant island edibles. Tabby ruins at

Fort Frederica tell of the former, while an occasional shell mound or refuse pit hint of the latter.

In 1794, stands of live oak on the west side of the island were harvested and cut into timbers for building important new warships such as the USS *Constitution*, better known as "Old Ironsides." One hundred years later, huge sawmills carved cypress and long-leaf pine into lumber for shipment to ports scattered around the world. Facilitating this commerce, to the south stands one of Georgia's last remaining lighthouses, a silent sentinel overlooking the "Marshes of Glynn" made famous by Georgia poet Sidney Lanier.

The original lighthouse was an octagonal-shaped structure reaching skyward for 75 feet, its 25-foot-wide base tapering to just 10 feet in diameter near the top. The tower's highest 13 feet were built of resilient brick; the remainder was formed from tabby, a commonly used coastal concrete crafted from sand, lime, water, and oyster shells. The structure was capped with a 10-foot-tall iron and glass lantern assembly.

Builder James Gould, a native of Massachusetts, began the project in 1808. When the lighthouse was finally finished in 1811, Gould stayed on as its first keeper, a position he held until 1837. Daily, Gould would climb the many steps to the top of the tower. There he would carefully clean and polish the glass elements, trim the wicks, and refill the oil lamps.

When the Confederate troops were withdrawn from St. Simons in 1862, the lighthouse was destroyed to prevent its use by the Federal blockading squadron. After the war, a brick replacement was erected a short distance north of the original site. Designed by noted architect Charles B. Cluskey, the 104-foot-tall tower went into service on September 1, 1872. Today, more than a century later, the lighthouse remains in active use, throwing a beam 16 miles out to sea on a clear night.

Sapelo Island Lighthouse

Darien, Georgia, fifty miles south of Savannah, was a thriving seaport when the 19th century came to America. Strategically located on the mouth of the mighty Altamaha River, Darien's harbor specialized in the export of rice, cotton, and timber. To better protect the many steamers and sailing vessels plying coastal waters enroute to Darien, the United States Lighthouse Service contracted with Winslow Lewis, a retired sea captain from Boston, for the construction of a brick lighthouse on the south end of nearby Sapelo Island.

Lewis completed the lighthouse, along with an adjacent keeper's house, in 1820. The cone-shaped structure stood 65 feet high, its 25-foot base tapering to just 12 feet across at the top. For many years, Sapelo's light blazed steadily forth, safely guiding ships through the dangerous waters of Doboy Sound, where the Altamaha joins the Atlantic Ocean.

During the Civil War, many of Georgia's coastal signposts were intentionally destroyed to prevent their use by invading Federal forces. Although Sapelo's light and reflector system were demolished, the tower itself was spared. When shipping traffic resumed after the war, a new lantern assembly was quickly installed, and Sapelo's light again pierced the night air.

In October of 1898, the eye of a hurricane winked at Sapelo with devastating effect. As a huge tidal surge more than 12 feet above normal swept over the island, storm-driven breakers lashed furiously at the base of the lighthouse, seriously undermining its foundation. Although a portion of the brick keeper's house was torn down to shore up the flagging foundation, the tower's continued stability remained threatened. Consequently, the Lighthouse Service sought a replacement for the old beacon.

In 1905, a modern, steel-skeleton structure was erected, along with a pair of wood-frame keeper's residences, and the old lighthouse was abandoned. For 28 years, the new lighthouse safely guided mariners through Doboy Sound. Then, in 1933, when shipping traffic had declined to a mere trickle, the Sapelo station was officially closed. The steel tower was dismantled and removed for service elsewhere, and the twin keeper's cottages were sold for scrap lumber. The south end of the island was again deserted.

But the old brick tower with its rusty iron cupola still remains, defying both sea and time. Sapelo's silent sentinel has become a symbol of the past.

Chapter 3:

Timbered
Tunnels
Through
Time

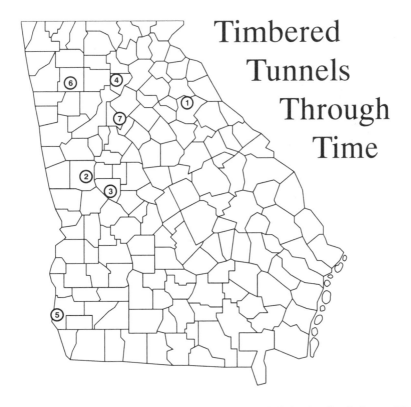

1 Watson Mill Covered Bridge   5 Coheelee Creek Covered Bridge
2 Red Oak Creek Covered Bridge   6 Lowry Covered Bridge
3 Auchumpkee Creek Covered Bridge   7 Stone Mountain Covered Bridge
4 Pool's Mill Covered Bridge

Watson Mill
Covered Bridge

There is a certain sense of tranquility, a serenity almost touching upon euphoria, associated with Georgia's covered bridges. Transcending time itself, these timbered tunnels tell of bygone days when life seemed much simpler, gentler, and slower-paced. Once numbering in the hundreds, today less than a score remain standing, victims of floods, fires, and progress.

One of Georgia's best-known covered bridges spans the south fork of the Broad River near Carlton in northeastern Georgia. Named for a now-vanished gristmill operated by Gabriel Watson in the late 1800s, this wooden masterpiece has carried traffic between Madison and Oglethorpe counties for over 100 years.

Watson Mill Covered Bridge consists of three wooden spans supported by a unique lattice truss designed by a Connecticut Yankee named Ithiel Town. Patented in 1820, Town's novel truss consists of a web of plain planks held firmly together with wooden pins, much resembling a gigantic garden trellis. Strong, yet simple and inexpensive to build, Town's design ushered in a new era of American bridge-building.

Most of the timbers comprising the century-old, weatherboarded structure are original, a lasting tribute to seasoned builder, Washington W. King. Born on January 22, 1843, Washington was the oldest son of Georgia's master bridge builder, Horace King. Operating out of LaGrange, the King family erected a number of fine bridges in Georgia, Alabama, and Mississippi.

The Civil War took a heavy toll on covered bridges in the South. Some were burned by Federals to hamper movement of Southern troops and supplies; many others were put to the torch by retreating Confederates to hinder the Federal advance. During the days of Reconstruction, Horace and his sons maintained a feverish pace rebuilding these war-wrecked bridges.

Washington eventually moved to Atlanta, where he started his own company and established his own superb bridge-building reputation. Among the many contracts he received was one for the construction of a covered bridge at Watson Mill in 1885.

With a length of nearly 230 feet, Watson Mill Covered Bridge carries the distinction of being Georgia's longest remaining covered bridge. Carefully engineered and executed, the bridge's construction has withstood the test of time, outliving both the old Watson Mill and a small hydroelectric plant built just downstream in 1905. Hugging the very water which gives it life, this magnificent bridge continues to defy the clements which have claimed many lesser structures.

Red Oak Creek
Covered Bridge

One of Georgia's finest covered bridges lies tucked away in the woods of Meriwether County, on an unpaved road east of Georgia highway 85 roughly midway between Woodbury and Gay. The old wooden structure, flanked by a rich forest of oak, spans the often unpredictable waters of Red Oak Creek. Seemingly tethering time, Red Oak Creek Bridge takes visitors on a passage through history to the days of the Antebellum South.

The man responsible for constructing this magnificent hooded crossing was Horace King, Georgia's master bridge builder. Born into bondage on September 8, 1807, King was "bought" by well-known builder and architect John Godwin when his first master died in 1829. Godwin quickly recognized the young man's exceptional mechanical abilities and provided for a proper education.

In 1832, Godwin and King left their native South Carolina and moved to Girard (now called Phenix City), Alabama. There, the talented duo built an elaborate covered bridge across the wide and wild Chattahoochee River. This bridge was the first in the region to employ a Town lattice truss assembly, a simple but sturdy network of crisscrossed planks fastened together with wooden pins. The immediate success of their first major bridge project launched King on a bridge-building career that would span nearly 40 years.

When John Godwin granted Horace King his freedom in 1846, King formed his own family construction business. Operating out of LaGrange, Georgia, Horace and his sons built bridges throughout the Southeast, specializing in difficult crossings that often intimidated other builders.

The Red Oak Creek crossing was no exception. Here the creek's shallow banks and wide floodplain required a very long and sturdy bridge. Of the bridge's total length of nearly 400 feet, a single 116-foot-span, over the main creek bed, was covered. The span's carefully selected, massive timbers have withstood the test of time, making the Red Oak Creek Bridge one of the the oldest surviving covered bridges in Georgia.

Horace King never forgot the man who had made his success possible. When John Godwin died on February 26, 1859, King erected a monument "In lasting remembrance of the love and gratitude he felt for his lost friend and former master."

Auchumpkee Creek Covered Bridge

Before the modern era of steel and concrete, bridges had to be built from wood. To prevent the wooden roadway and superstructure from rapid decay, bridges were enclosed in a shell of clapboard siding and roofing shingles, both inexpensive and fairly easy to replace. During the boom of 19th century roadbuilding, these romantic hooded structures reached invitingly across many creeks, streams, and rivers in the United States.

Of the dozen or so covered bridges built by Warren J. Alford and Dr. James W. Herring around the turn of the century, only one remains standing today. Magnificently preserved, this timbered tunnel spans the Auchumpkee Creek in Upson County. For many years, the 121-foot-long bridge ferried travelers on old Allen Road across the creek's shallow, gurgling waters.

Dr. Herring was a skilled physician and an accomplished engineer. While serving as County Commissioner in the 1890s, Dr. Herring designed many wooden bridges for Upson County.

Warren Alford was born on November 6, 1862. His father was killed early in the Civil War, leaving Warren's mother to provide for her six children. Dr. Herring befriended the struggling family and helped them through the troubled economic times that followed the war. He provided for Warren's education and taught him the construction skills he would later use in erecting covered bridges. Their extremely close relationship lasted until January 14, 1911, when Dr. Herring died at the age of 87.

One of middle Georgia's best-kept secrets, the Auchumpkee Creek Bridge was beautifully restored in 1976. The bridge is located just off U.S. 19 about 12 miles south of Thomaston.

Pool's Mill
Covered Bridge

The silt-laden waters of Settendown Creek roll lazily through the pine and poplar forests of the Appalachian foothills in northern Forsyth County. Past the small community of Heardville, about ten miles northwest of Cumming, the creek makes a sudden bend as it encounters a series of steep shoals. Hugging the banks just above the rapids, Pool's Mill Covered Bridge stands in splendid harmony with the environment. Branches bend low, gently brushing the water's surface. Myriad swirls speak of plentiful carp and bream. Deer, opossum, and raccoon leave their tracks in the soft mud along the low banks.

In the early part of the last century, this picturesque setting was owned by Chief George Welch, a mixed-blood Cherokee. Here he built a gristmill in the 1820s. Chief Welch lost both his land and mill in the 1832 Cherokee Gold Lottery — though he was later reimbursed $12,500 by the United States Government. After exchanging hands, the land was eventually sold to Dr. Marcus Lafayette Pool on February 17, 1870. Dr. Pool died in 1895, but the fine old structure which bears his name still ferries passersby on a trip through time.

The three-story combination gristmill-sawmill, with its large wooden wheel, disappeared long ago. Above the shoals, just below the bridge, a few iron rods protrude from the rock where the wooden dam once stood. Though not exquisitely preserved, the 90-year-old bridge remains standing, accessible to pedestrians and bicyclists.

When a spring freshet washed a previous bridge away in 1900, millwright John Wafford agreed to replace it. Planks of locally logged poplar poured from Pool's mill for the bridge's construction. These were neatly planed, cut to length, drilled, and piled beside the creek to await assembly.

Unfortunately, as Wafford soon discovered, the pieces to his 95-foot-long timbered tunnel did not fit together properly. He had somehow miscalculated and drilled the all-important holes for the interconnecting wooden pegs in the wrong places. Disgruntled, Wafford left the bridge unfinished. Another contractor stepped in, rebored the holes, and completed the project. To this day, the Pool's Mill Bridge carries the rather dubious distinction of being Georgia's only covered bridge with two sets of holes in each of its Town lattice timbers.

33

Coheelee Creek Covered Bridge

Early County in southwest Georgia carries a double distinction in historical significance. Prehistoric Indian mounds bulge from the ground at the northern tip of the county, and 15 miles to the southwest lies one of Georgia's few remaining covered bridges. With its distinguished weathered timbers, the century-old structure stretches 96 feet across colorful Coheelee Creek.

On May 2, 1883, the Early County Board of Commissioners appointed a special committee to determine whether a covered bridge should be built across the Coheelee Creek at a place called McDonald's Ford. After careful consideration, the committee recommended an alternate location over nearby Sowatchee Creek. The Board accepted the recommendation, and a bridge was soon built across the Sowatchee.

Eight years later, the Commissioners were again approached by local residents in favor of a bridge spanning the Coheelee. This time the Board acquiesced and a contract was let in 1891. Construction quickly commenced and progressed at a feverish pace: three dozen workers finished the entire bridge, from foundation to shingles, in just four months. Total cost of the project was $490.41.

While many other hooded crossings, including the Sowatchee, succumbed to the ravages of time long ago, the Coheelee Creek crossing remains in excellent condition to this day. Magnificently preserved, the bridge is located on Old River Road about two miles north of Hilton.

Lowry Covered Bridge

With the Bowen Electric Power Plant looming in the distance, Lowry Covered Bridge gracefully spans Euharlee Creek off Georgia Highway 113 west of Cartersville. Now closed to vehicular traffic, the old bridge vividly recalls a long and pleasant past.

The 116-foot-long weatherboarded structure, built of heartwood pine for added strength and durability, rests upon native stone piers 13 feet high. With the exception of a modern tin roof, the bridge appears today much as it did years ago when local miller Daniel Lowry supervised its construction.

Lowry's mill was located just a few paces from the bridge. When a freak flash flood swept a previous bridge away, it was Lowry who sought a replacement. Although Lowry's mill has long since crumbled to dust, his beautifully designed bridge has ably withstood the passage of time.

Stone Mountain Covered Bridge

What is now the Stone Mountain Covered Bridge originally spanned the north fork of the Oconee River in Athens, some 60 miles distant. Built by Washington W. King in 1892 for less than $2,500, the 151-foot bridge incorporated a simple Town Lattice in three spans. Known as the College Avenue Bridge for nearly three-quarters of a century, the old timbered structure was purchased by the Stone Mountain Memorial Association in 1964. The bridge was moved to its new home the following year at a cost of $18,000. Today, the noble structure spans a portion of Stone Mountain Park, providing nostalgic access to Indian Island.

Chapter 4:

Grist
for
the
Mill

1 Hamburg Mill
2 Watson Mill
3 Cochran Mills

4 Prater's Mill
5 Berry College's Old Mill

Hamburg Mill

Nearly a century ago, the Georgia plains were peppered with gristmills, dutifully crushing wheat into flour and corn into grits and meal. Many of these mills have not survived the passage of time. Some were pushed aside for housing developments or shopping malls. Others were destroyed by vandals; their secrets looted for eternity. And still others were simply left to rust, rot, and ruin.

One exception is the marvelously preserved Hamburg Mill on the Little Ogeechee River in northern Washington County. Built in 1921 by the Gilmore brothers of Agricola, Georgia, and now

40

protected as part of Hamburg State Park, the water-powered gristmill is still operating today. It was the second mill to be erected at this locale.

The first gristmill was built in 1850 by Richard Warthen, a native of North Carolina. Warthen's simple wooden dam and rather crude mill were located about 100 feet above the present mill site. Warthen rather optimistically named his mill after the Great Market in Hamburg, South Carolina, just across the river from Augusta. The frontier trading post of Georgetown lay six miles below Hamburg on the main branch of the Ogeechee. Indians from as far west as Alabama would journey to Georgetown to trade, which sometimes included bartering for Warthen's grits and corn meal.

While Warthen's old mill was powered by a conventional water wheel, the Gilmore brothers opted for a much smaller, but more powerful, water turbine instead. The turbine, which sits at the bottom of a well-type shaft, has a spirally shaped core. Water from the millpond flows down the shaft and into the turbine, causing the rotor to spin, thus generating the mill's power. At Hamburg, the core is connected to the mill's three sets of grinding stones by a series of metal shafts, reduction gears, and long leather belts.

The grinding surfaces of the stones are faced with a number of sloping radial grooves which become shallower as they approach the outer edge. When the top stone is slowly rotated above the stationary bottom stone, the grooves cross in a scissors-like fashion, providing the necessary grinding action. Kernels of corn, dropped from a hopper through a hole in the upper stone, are cracked near the center and then ground progressively finer as they are pushed to the outer edge.

One of the few surviving gristmills in Georgia, Hamburg Mill is faithfully preserving this important facet of Americana for future generations.

42

Watson Mill

Watson Mill, located on Fifteen Mile Creek just a dozen miles east of Swainsboro, is one of the most unique historical structures still standing in Georgia. The remarkable, century-old building combines both a gristmill and a covered bridge under a single spacious roof.

Construction of the mill began in 1880. While some workers dumped heaping wheelbarrows of dirt into the slowly growing earthen dam, others dropped huge trees in the nearby forests. Trimmed of their limbs, the logs were floated down the creek to the construction site, where they were sliced into appropriate sized timbers. Sturdy mortise and tenon construction, typically used for barns and other large wooden structures, was employed throughout the mill housing.

Below the mill, 32 wooden floodgates regulated water depth in the cypress-filled reservoir, originally called Hendricks and Parish's Pond for the first mill owners. A single turbine, later supplemented with the power of a diesel engine, turned three sets of stones in the gristmill and a gin for separating seed from precious cotton fibers.

Hubert Watson, for whom the mill and pond are now named, bought the property in 1943. For over 30 years Watson ran a successful business, attracting loyal customers from many miles away. In 1975, the site was purchased by the State of Georgia, and historic Watson Mill was preserved as part of the newly created George L. Smith State Park.

Cochran Mills

Sometime in the early 1800s, a man named Cheadle Cochran settled on a farm between the growing towns of Palmetto and Campbellton, in what is now part of South Fulton County. Becoming a leading citizen, Cochran went on to a prestigious career as a state senator, playing a major role in legislating mail routes in Georgia. Working the land in addition to working for the land, Cochran was also an assiduous farmer and miller. When he died in 1854, his estate included 700 acres of land, 40 slaves, and a rustic gristmill located on Little Bear Creek.

One of Cochran's sons, Owen, took over operation of his father's mill. For many years, Owen's mill ground countless bushels of wheat into barrels of flour, and crushed innumerable baskets of corn into sacks of meal, grits, and feed. But today, precious little remains of the once prosperous mill.

The mill's wooden structures were burned by vandals in 1967. A few stone columns and patchy wall segments still abut the creek, and portions of rusty iron penstock lie broken and twisted along the adjoining hillside. Originally 80 feet long, the mill's fieldstone dam was dynamited by vandals just a few years ago.

To reach the ruins, located just a few hundred feet off present-day Cochran Mill Road, visitors must first walk over an old steel and wood truss bridge. The bridge dates to the latter half of the 19th century and carried traffic along the old Cochran Mill Road.

In 1870, Owen's older brother Berry built a small mill on the main branch of Bear Creek. Like the other Cochran site, Berry's wood-framed gristmill was destroyed by vandals in 1972. The 48-foot-long fieldstone dam remains intact, however, and even retains part of a cleaning sluice and fragments of penstock. This old and interesting dam may be reached from the Owen Cochran mill site by following a dirt path (part of the old Cochran Mill Road) for about half a mile.

The property has changed hands several times over the years, at one time belonging to Dr. Hiram Evans, head of the Ku Klux Klan. During the 1940s, Evans isolated the property by erecting a high electrified fence along its border. To provide power for the fence and other facilities, Evans constructed a large reinforced-concrete dam downstream from the old Berry Cochran dam. A sluice carried water to a generator house located on an adjacent hillslope. Evans also built a wooden pavilion in the large pond formed by the new dam. But exactly what Evans and his fellow Klan members did on the property has remained hooded in mystery.

Today, the land once again belongs to the people. The old dams, bridges, and mill ruins, in their tranquil and scenic settings, are now part of the Fulton County Parks System.

Prater's Mill

In 1858, Benjamin Prater and Tilmond Pitner purchased a sawmill and 80 acres of land in Whitfield County, strategically situated where the local wagon road crossed over Coahulla Creek. The commercial establishment that soon grew up alongside the creek became one of the largest integrated mills in north Georgia. At its peak, Prater's Mill included a gristmill, sawmill, cotton gin, wool corder, blacksmith shop, general store, and hotel.

Because grinding was normally performed on a first-come, first-served basis, the prudent farmer would rise before dawn in order to beat the crowd. Younger children would often accompany him to the mill, where they would fish, swim, or merely soak in the sights and sounds while the grain was being ground. At Prater's, farmers could tend to other chores — such as stocking up on necessary provisions or repairing broken tools — while they waited. Or they might simply relax; discussing the weather or politics, or spinning yarns — all welcome diversions from the normal obligations on the farm.

Prater's Mill served the community for nearly a century before finally closing its doors in the early 1950s. Well maintained and still functional, the old mill is operated occasionally during the spring and fall in connection with an arts and crafts festival held on the site. A portion of the past which is alive today, Prater's Mill is located on Georgia Highway 2, about ten miles north of Dalton.

Berry College's Old Mill

Rome, Georgia, where the rolling waters of the Etowah and Oostanaula rivers join to form the mighty Coosa, is home to beautiful Berry College. The world's largest college campus, Berry also sports one of the world's largest water wheels. Tucked into the tall pine woods in a far corner of the campus, the 42-foot-diameter wooden water wheel has ground Berry-grown grain into meal and grits for over half a century.

The wheel's immense iron hub once served in a similar capacity at nearby Hermitage, an early northwest Georgia manufacturing complex. Donated by The Republic Mining and Manufacturing Company, the gigantic hub was transported to its new home in 1930 by automobile magnate Henry Ford. Student workers then carefully rebuilt the huge wheel and constructed the natural-rock mill complex. Water, gravity-fed from Berry's own reservoir, still powers the Old Mill.

Chapter 5:

Early
Industry
and
Trade

1 Columbus Iron Works
2 Confederate Powder Works
3 Cooper Iron Works
4 Central of Georgia Railway Roundhouse
5 Augusta Cotton Exchange
6 Butler Island Plantation
7 McIntosh Sugar Works

Columbus Iron Works

Walking through the doorway of the Columbus Convention and Trade Center is like stepping back in time. What once appeared old has been made to seem new again. The massive timbers and brickwork remain unchanged from the past century. Even the shafts and pulleys still hang from the ceiling, as if suspended in time. Through skillful melding of past and present, the historic structure of the Columbus Iron Works has been preserved for the future.

Located on the Georgia bank of the Chattahoochee River, the Columbus Iron Works began operation in 1853. For over a century, the factory produced a variety of cast iron products, including syrup kettles, farm implements, and steam engines. During the Civil War, the factory was a major supplier of cannons for the Confederacy.

The Columbus Iron Works also manufactured boilers and steam engines for the Confederate navy. When the C.S.S. *Jackson*, a 225-foot ironclad ram, was built at the nearby navy yard, the Iron Works supplied the two-inch thick iron plating which protected the vessel's wooden hull.

In April 1865, unaware that General Robert E. Lee had surrendered just one week earlier, General James H. Wilson's Union cavalry swept across Alabama toward Georgia, wreaking death and destruction. On the night of April 16, Columbus fell in what would be the last significant battle of the Civil War. Captured the following day, the *Jackson* was torched and set adrift. The vessel grounded on a sandbar some 30 miles downriver and slowly burned to her water line. Salvaged one hundred years later, the *Jackson*'s remains are now housed at the Confederate Naval Museum, just a short distance from the Iron Works.

After the war, the Iron Works continued to produce a wide variety of fine cast iron and other metal products. From 1880 until the 1920s, the company manufactured a highly successful commercial ice-making machine. But modern foundry and manufacturing techniques finally made the old building obsolete. Fortunately, in 1976 the site was selected as the home of the city's new Convention and Trade Center. Converted into a unique meeting and exhibit facility while retaining its link to the past, the fine old building has entered a new era of usefulness.

Confederate
Powder Works

Near downtown Augusta, between the Savannah River and the Augusta Canal, stands a majestic brick obelisk called the Confederate Chimney. Towering 176 feet high, the chimney is all that remains of an enormous gunpowder manufacturing plant built during the Civil War. Here the necessary ingredients of charcoal, sulfur, and saltpeter were carefully crushed, mixed, ground, and compressed into explosive powder for Confederate muskets and cannons.

On July 10, 1861, President Jefferson Davis assigned to Colonel George Washington Rains the critical task of developing what would become the South's largest powder works. After touring dozens of potential sites, Rains selected a 240-acre tract of land along the banks of the Augusta Canal. In addition to its strategic central location, the Augusta site offered abundant water power, ample railroad facilities, and security from Union attack.

Construction began in September and continued at a feverish pace, consuming more than five million clay bricks and a train-load of granite from Georgia's Stone Mountain. Machinery for the works came from all over the Confederacy. Massive rollers, bed plates, and hydraulic presses arrived from Virginia, while huge shafts and gears came from Tennessee. Foundries and machine shops in Georgia, Louisiana, and North and South Carolina supplied other vital pieces of machinery. When completed, the 26 buildings composing the new Confederate Powder Works stretched along the canal banks for nearly two miles.

The immense manufacturing complex began operating in April of 1862. The plant quickly paid for itself and saved the Confederate government many millions of dollars by producing powder at far less cost than could be purchased through the blockade. By the end of the war, the Confederate Powder Works had produced nearly 2.75 million pounds of gunpowder.

No longer needed, the machinery was scrapped after the war and the unique cluster of brick buildings demolished. During the 1880s, the stately Sibley Cotton Mill was erected upon the site, its elegant brick facade reminiscent of the former powder works. But the original factory chimney still remains, a lasting memorial to the thousands of Southern soldiers who died during the American Civil War.

Cooper Iron Works

Just downstream from the Allatoona Dam on the Etowah River, three miles from Cartersville in Bartow County, stands the ruin of the Cooper Iron Works. Owned by Georgia congressman and entrepreneur Mark Anthony Cooper, the iron works was, at one time, North Georgia's premier industrial complex. Destroyed by Federal forces during the Civil War, all that remains of the immense manufacturing center is a thirty-foot-tall mortared mound of rock that was once a bustling blast furnace.

In the late 1830s, the town of Etowah, Georgia, was founded by Jacob Stroup, whose son Moses built a blast furnace nearby and began a small-scale milling and manufacturing operation. Cooper purchased the blast furnace in 1847, and quickly made it the center of a large industrial complex which included a rolling mill, foundry, and spike and nail factory. Cooper also erected a large gristmill capable of grinding 300 barrels of flour per day.

To shuttle freight between the iron works and the Western and Atlantic Railroad at Etowah Crossing four miles away, Cooper constructed his own spur track. The little switch engine Yonah, which routinely rode those rails, played an important role in the "Great Locomotive Chase" during the Civil War. If not for the Yonah, the Federals may have succeeded in their daring attempt to steal a train and disrupt Confederate supply lines by burning bridges while racing north.

The blast furnace which dominated the Cooper Iron Works operated much like a gigantic blacksmith's forge. The intense heat created by forcing blasts of air from a water-powered bellows through burning charcoal melted a mixture of iron ore and limestone. The molten limestone absorbed impurities from the iron and rose to the top to be skimmed off as slag. The molten iron sank to the bottom where it flowed into molds resembling a mother pig feeding her young. (Hence the term "pig iron.") The blast furnace operated nearly continuously throughout the year, producing an average of 25 tons of pig iron each week.

Located a few hundred yards upstream, Allatoona Dam offers a stark contrast between old and new. Begun in 1941, but interrupted by the outbreak of World War II, the dam's construction was finally finished in January 1950, after consuming nearly half a million yards of concrete. Standing 190 feet tall and 1,250 feet long, the dam impounds a 12,000-acre lake with over 270 miles of shoreline, and annually generates more than 140 million kilowatt-hours of electricity.

The once-thriving town of Etowah, with houses, stores, and hotels stretching for a mile up the winding river, shared the life, and death, of the Cooper Iron Works. When General Sherman's forces arrived in 1864, both town and iron works were put to the torch, never to be rebuilt.

Although the ghost town of Etowah now lies buried under the deep waters of Lake Allatoona, the old blast furnace remains on its original site, part of the Cooper Furnace Day Use Area owned and operated by the U.S. Army Corps of Engineers.

Central of Georgia Railway Roundhouse

Located at 601 West Harris Street near downtown Savannah, the Central of Georgia Railway Roundhouse was the repair and maintenance center for the company's locomotives. Built before the Civil War, today the roundhouse resembles the ruins of an ancient Roman coliseum. Managed by the Coastal Heritage Society, the historic site remains a lasting tribute to early railroading in America.

During 1834, the newly chartered Central Railroad and Canal Company conducted a survey to determine the feasibility and cost of constructing a railroad from seaside Savannah to the central commerce capital of Macon. Two years later, the Central Railroad of Georgia (later renamed the Central of Georgia Railway) was formed, and construction of the proposed line began. William W. Gordon, mayor of Savannah and firm supporter of the railroad, became the company's first president. By October of 1843 the 190-mile-long rail line was finished, with regular passenger service between the two cities beginning on November 1.

Sprawling over five acres, the roundhouse complex included more than a dozen buildings devoted to the care and upkeep of locomotives and rolling stock. At the very center of the roundhouse sat a sturdy turntable. This gigantic "lazy Susan" for railroads would rotate the locomotives and tenders around a central pivot point, directing them to the appropriate work bay or maintenance pit. At first the simple platform could be moved manually, but as locomotives grew larger and heavier over the years, and the turntable was enlarged to accommodate them, electric motors became a necessity.

For over a hundred years the roundhouse complex was a hub of activity as workers crawled over, under, and sometimes through their iron horses, preparing them for the long journeys ahead. There were axles to grease, boilers to inspect, and fireboxes to clean and maintain. Blacksmith shops rang with the sharp clang of metal striking metal, while carpenter shops buzzed to the sound of saws biting into wood.

But as the era of the great steam locomotive finally drew to a close, the workers went on to other tasks, and the Central of Georgia Railway Roundhouse became a page of the past.

Augusta Cotton Exchange

Augusta, gracefully spread along the Georgia bank of the Savannah River, has long been associated with the cotton industry. From the growth of raw cotton fiber to the manufacture of colorful yarn and cloth, Augusta has played a major role, being at one time the second largest inland cotton market in the world. During the frenetic days of the cotton boom, over 200 members joined the Augusta Cotton Exchange, a market organization for buying and selling cotton that stretched across the globe.

Located downtown on the corner of Eighth and Reynolds Streets, the Cotton Exchange Building was constructed in 1886 to house the business activities of brokering cotton. The beautiful Victorian structure provided ample office space for brokers and a broad trading floor where buyers and sellers could closely monitor the daily price fluctuations of cotton and other commodities. The Augusta Cotton Exchange occupied the building until 1964.

For the next 24 years the building sat vacant, suffering from vandalism and neglect. Beginning in 1988, the old building was authentically restored in a painstaking process which cost over 80 times more than the original construction. Today, the historic structure houses a unique welcome center and museum.

A permanent display leads visitors from the planting and harvesting of cotton to turn-of-the-century manufacturing processes. Many of the items, including a huge 45-foot blackboard for posting daily market quotes and a long wooden counter for telegraph operators, were originally used in the Cotton Exchange Building during its days of operations. These and other reminders from the past, from farm implements to bale scales, hark back to a very busy time when cotton was truly king.

Butler Island Plantation

When cotton was king, rice was surely queen — at least in 19th century McIntosh County. Jutting from the marsh along US 17 little more than a mile south of Darien, the remains of an old brick kiln and a 75-foot chimney bear testimony to the importance of rice production along Georgia's antebellum coast. Built by slaves in the 1850s, the relics were once part of a huge rice mill on the famous Butler Island Rice Plantation.

Butler Island — actually a delta formed by the Altamaha River — was purchased late in the 18th century by Major Pierce Butler, an officer in the British Army. Butler, who resigned before the Revolutionary War, married a South Carolina heiress, and developed his Georgia rice plantation into a highly profitable business. When Butler died in 1822, his land passed to his grandson and namesake. Under the care and supervision of the younger Pierce Butler, the plantation continued to prosper, yielding healthy harvests of Georgian rice.

In 1834 Pierce Butler married the beautiful and talented English actress Frances Anne (Fanny) Kemble. The couple settled in Philadelphia, but Pierce regularly visited Georgia to manage the rice plantation. During the winter of 1838-39, Pierce was accompanied by his wife and their two small children. Fashionable and impetuous, Fanny soon grew bored with life in the South. She left Georgia in the spring, never to return. A few years later she left her husband and returned to England. But Fanny Kemble was to have a permanent impact upon the South.

Opposed to slavery, the young actress had vividly recorded her thoughts and impressions in the form of a diary during her brief stay. Fanny's *Journal of a Residence on a Georgian Plantation*, published in 1863, is said to have helped sway public opinion in England against the Confederacy during the Civil War.

Although his sympathies lay with the South, Pierce Butler remained in his native Philadelphia throughout the four years of bitter civil war. In 1866, Butler returned to the plantation and attempted to restore it to its former prosperity. But the old way of life was simply no longer possible; this part of the South would not, could not, be reconstructed.

In 1954 the historic plantation was acquired by the State of Georgia and eventually became part of the Altamaha Wildfowl Area. Today, the vast acreage painstakingly cleared by Butler's slaves has returned to marshland. Originally dug to help drain the swampy but fertile soil, the old canals now provide convenient access for hunters and other outdoorsmen.

McIntosh Sugar Works

In the early 19th century, a middle-aged entrepreneur named John McIntosh erected a sugar factory on his plantation in Camden County, near the town of St. Marys. This novel sugar house was run by slaves and employed the first animal-powered horizontal mill brought to Georgia. For many years this large-scale sugar manufactory sweetened the lives of consumers up and down the coast. Today, the nearly forgotten factory's tabby ruins lie at the intersection of Spur 40 and Kings Bay Road, across the highway from the main entrance to the Kings Bay Naval Submarine Support Base.

John Houstoun McIntosh was born in 1773 in what is now McIntosh County, but moved to Spanish-owned Florida as a young man. There, during the War of 1812, McIntosh and a band of loyal followers attempted to free Florida from Spanish rule. Their efforts failed, however, and McIntosh returned to his native Georgia after the war.

McIntosh settled on the Marianna Plantation, located near the mouth of the St. Marys River. In 1819, he purchased additional acreage which he named the New Canaan Plantation. This land was soon cultivated in sugar cane. His immense sugar works was constructed shortly thereafter.

The rectangular-shaped factory was built from tabby and consisted of three large rooms. In one room sat the horizontal roller mill which squeezed the juice from the sugar cane. Another room contained wood-fired furnaces and kettles used for boiling the juice into a thick syrup, which was then poured into huge vats to cool and crystallize. The finished sugar was packaged and hauled to St. Marys for shipping.

McIntosh's sugar factory long outlived its builder, and the property exchanged hands several times after his death. When sugar production finally ceased many years ago, much of the original equipment was salvaged and put to use elsewhere. Gutted by fire, all that now remain are the slowly crumbling tabby walls, and many memories handed down through time.

Chapter 6:

The Best
Dam Sites
in Georgia

1 High Falls Dam   4 Tallulah Falls Dam
2 Morgan Falls Hydroelectric Plant   5 Tugalo Dam
3 Lloyd Shoals Hydroelectric Plant

High Falls Dam

Historic High Falls Dam is located in Monroe County approximately 50 miles south of Atlanta and just a stone's throw off Interstate 75. The dam, built in 1905 and used for electrical power generation until 1958, backs up the Towaliga River into a shallow 700-acre lake. But the waters of the Towaliga are stayed only briefly. Cresting the dam's main 400-foot spillway, they continue to tumble over waterfalls and rapids in their headlong rush to the Ocmulgee, the Altamaha, and finally the Atlantic Ocean.

The purling waters of the Towaliga were first harnessed by a gristmill built before the Civil War. Burned by retreating Confederate soldiers to prevent stored supplies from falling into enemy hands, the mill was rebuilt in 1866, and a town sprang up in its shadow. The town was named High Falls, after a nearby scenic but tortuous stretch of river which quickly dropped more than 100 feet.

During its heyday from 1883-1889, the town sported a saw-mill, cotton mill, factories for manufacturing shoes, brooms, and furniture, a blacksmith shop, general store, and post office. But when the railroad bypassed High Falls in favor of Jackson, eight miles to the east, a death knell sounded for the small town. Mail delivery came to a halt in the early 1900s, and the town quietly faded into history. Even the old gristmill, located on the south side of the Towaliga about 400 feet downstream of the dam, succumbed to the sands of time.

In 1898, the Towaliga Power Company purchased some of the land around High Falls and constructed the dam and generating facilities in 1905. The 600-foot-long, 35-foot-high dam is of stone and mortar construction: the stone blocks were cut from the streambed below the dam. When in operation, lake water was diverted into a canal and penstock system to a hydroelectric power plant located about 1,600 feet downstream.

On October 27, 1958, after 53 years of continuous service, the power plant was shut down for economic reasons. A few years later the dam and surrounding parcels of land were donated to the State of Georgia. High Falls State Park was established shortly thereafter.

Morgan Falls
Hydroelectric Power
Plant

Sixteen miles north of Atlanta, at a place once called Bull Sluice, the waters of the Chattahoochee River slap against the formidable bulk of Morgan Falls Dam. Buttressed by walls of solid rock on each side of the river, the 900-foot-long by 50-foot-high masonry dam diverts the Chattahoochee's flow to a hydroelectric plant nestled against the river's east bank. Completed in 1904, this historic power plant is still in operation, using much of the original generating equipment.

The Morgan Falls Hydroelectric Power Plant was the brain-child of inventor and entrepreneur S. Morgan Smith. Born in North Carolina in 1839, Smith had spent most of his life in Pennsylvania before venturing back south and into Georgia. Around the turn of the century, Smith recognized the enormous potential for hydroelectric power along the Chattahoochee River. He formed the Atlanta Water and Electric Power Company and began planning what would become the South's largest hydro-electric facility at that time. The Georgia Railway and Electric Company (later to become the Georgia Power Company) agreed to purchase all electricity produced at the new site.

Construction began in September of 1902. Huge stone slabs for the body of the dam were hewn from quarries located on either side of the river immediately above the dam. Sand for mortar was dredged from the river bed below the dam.

The elegant powerhouse, an impressive 196 feet long, 40 feet wide, and 30 feet tall, is built of brick. Within, seven turbines, each direct-coupled to a 1,500 kilowatt generator, convert the mechanical energy of falling water into electricity.

Morgan Smith died a year before his massive project was completed. But engineered and built to last, the Morgan Falls Hydroelectric Power Plant continues operating to this day, pro-viding more than 87 years of uninterrupted, dependable service.

Lloyd Shoals Hydroelectric Plant

Picturesque Lloyd Shoals Hydroelectric Plant is nestled in a narrow river valley between Butts and Jasper counties, eight miles from Jackson. Here, waters from the South, Yellow, and Alcovy rivers meet to form Jackson Lake, and spilling through the dam, continue on their way as the awesome Ocmulgee. When built shortly after the turn of the century, the imposing dam was described as a "striking example of the thrift, enterprise, and rapid development of the New South."

The contract for the dam's construction was awarded by the Central Georgia Power Company (which later merged with the Georgia Power Company) on September 14, 1908. To facilitate movement of men and materials, a six-mile-long "Dam Short Line" was laid to the nearest point on the Southern Railroad. Temporary timber trestles were erected across deep ravines, raging rapids, and wide streams. By October, construction was in full swing.

A steady supply of sand for the dam's construction was dredged from the bed of the Ocmulgee, while stone was quarried from the nearby granite cliffs and crushed at the site. The sand and stone were mixed with cement to form concrete; some 160,000 cubic yards were poured during the project. The completed dam stood 100 feet high, stretched 1,070 feet between valley walls, and was 90 feet thick at the base.

The power house, a 200-foot-long two-story structure, was built directly into the dam. Four generators were initially installed; two additional units were added later. Still operating today with much of the original equipment, the plant's hydroelectric power is distributed throughout North-Central Georgia.

Tallulah Falls Dam

Northeast Georgia is an enchanted land of roaring waterfalls, gurgling rapids, and whispering streams. Years ago, a mighty river flowed fast and furious across the land, tumbling over the twisted bedrock which forms the foothills of the Blue Ridge Mountains. The Cherokee Indians called the river "Tallulah," meaning "terrible," for the countless cataracts and impassable rapids found along its path. Early settlers caught the spirit, naming many scenic splendors along a tremendous gash in the earth known as Tallulah Gorge. Visitors came from near and far to admire the river's tumultuous torrents, but the Tallulah's destiny soon took a different course.

For centuries, the natural energy of falling water had been harnessed by simple mechanical wheels at innumerable gristmills and factories throughout the world. During the late 1800s, however, the production of hydroelectric power became practical, along with the ability to transmit electricity over long distances. Suddenly, instead of taking the factories to the rivers, the power of the river could conveniently be brought to the factory. To meet the ever-growing demand for hydroelectric power, huge dams were erected to store the vast quantities of water needed to produce a large, steady stream of electricity.

One such dam is located at Tallulah Falls, midway between Clayton and Clarkesville on highway 441. Standing 126 feet high and 426 feet long, Tallulah Falls Dam is the oldest and largest of six dams built in stair-step fashion on a 28-mile stretch of the Tallulah and Tugaloo Rivers by the Georgia Railway and Power Company (predecessor to the Georgia Power Company). When completed in 1913, the dam's generating capacity of 72,000 kilowatts made it the third largest hydroelectric facility in the country for many years.

By locating the dam's power plant more than a mile downstream from the dam itself, chief engineer Charles O. Lenz substantially increased the water's fall to just over 600 feet. A tunnel 11 feet wide and 14 feet high, hewn through 6,666 feet of solid rock, directs impounded lake water to the side of the gorge above the powerhouse. From there, six massive steel penstocks, five feet in diameter and 1,200 feet long, carry the water to the generators below.

When construction began in 1911, not everyone wanted to see the river harnessed and the natural beauty of the gorge

75

compromised. Despite heroic attempts to halt the dam's construction, led by the widow of Confederate General James Longstreet, the project continued on course. In September of 1913, the river was diverted into the tunnel and powerhouse far below, the giant turbines began spinning, and electricity flowed over newly strung wires to fuel factories and homes in the growing metropolis of Atlanta. Over the next 13 years, five more dams would be built along the river.

But there was a cost associated with the coming of the electrical age to Northeast Georgia. Beautiful Ladore Falls, majestic Hurricane Falls, and temperamental Tempesta Falls vanished, buried under thousands of acre-feet of manmade reservoirs. Gone, also, were Horseshoe Bend, Indian Arrow Rapids, Witch's Head, and dozens of other special places with fanciful names. The "terrible" Tallulah had been tamed.

Tugalo Dam

Three miles southeast of the Tallulah Falls Dam sits the second largest and second oldest facility in Georgia Power's North Georgia Hydro Group. Named Tugalo for the Cherokee word meaning "fork of a stream," the dam is located just downstream of where the Tallulah and Chattooga rivers meet to form the Tugalo River. Spanning 940 feet, the 153-foot-tall dam holds back Lake Tugalo, a 600-acre reservoir with a shoreline stretching over 18 miles.

Construction of the Tugalo Dam began in 1917 but soon stopped due to the poor financial climate following World War I. Work feverishly resumed in January of 1922. By the end of 1923, the plant's first two generators were producing electricity, followed by the other two generators the next year.

Like the Tallulah Falls Dam to the north, Tugalo's generators are directly coupled to individual water wheels. Still operating today, Tugalo's four generators produce a total of 45,000 kilowatts of clean, gravity-fed hydroelectric power.

Chapter 7:

Georgia Potpourri

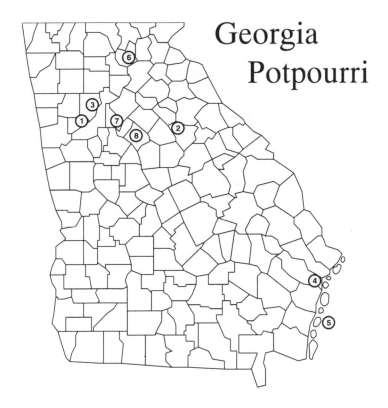

1 Sweetwater Creek Ruins
2 Scull Shoals Ruins
3 Sope Creek Ruins
4 Sunbury

5 Christ Church
6 Dahlonega Gold Museum
7 Stone Mountain Carving
8 Porterdale Mills

Sweetwater Creek Ruins

On the west bank of Sweetwater Creek in eastern Douglas County, the ruins of a water-powered textile mill stand in stark testimony to the ravages of war. Here, during a brief heartbeat of the Civil War, a mill was destroyed, a town burned to the ground, and its inhabitants driven from the land.

In the mid-1840s, Governor Charles McDonald and Colonel James Rogers established the Sweetwater Manufacturing Company to produce a variety of cotton goods and also to grind grain into flour. The massive five-story mill was finally completed and went into production on December 21, 1849. Eight years later, the company's name was changed to the New Manchester Manufacturing Company.

The mill bustled with activity, dominating life in the nearby town of New Manchester. Workers toiled from sunup to sundown, spinning cotton into thread and weaving thread into fabric. Production progressed at a feverish pace throughout the year, halting only for essential repairs or occasional periods of low water. At such times, the mill served as impromptu meeting hall, dance floor, and even wedding chapel.

To power the huge factory, a 300-foot-long wooden dam, erected on a naturally occurring rock ledge, backed up the creek and diverted water into a stone-lined millrace running along the bank. Several hundred yards downstream, the murky water passed through a large stone arch and over a massive water wheel. A single vertical shaft connected the water wheel to all floors, where simple networks of belts and pulleys turned spinning frames, looms, and other pieces of machinery.

For nearly 15 years, the mill's water wheel creaked and groaned beside the tumbling cascades of Sweetwater Creek. Then, early on Saturday morning, July 2, 1864, Federal troops under Major Haviland Thompkins suddenly surrounded New Manchester and shut down the mill, which had been busily churning out war-time goods for the Confederacy. Despite a week of desperate pleading, the townspeople were evacuated on July 9 and the mill and town unceremoniously put to the torch.

Today, portions of the old millrace and fragmented factory walls are all that remain: traces of the town have long since melted into the forest floor. Such was the tragedy of Sweetwater, a casualty of General William T. Sherman's march to Atlanta and to the sea beyond.

Scull Shoals Ruins

Scull Shoals, situated on the Oconee River about 12 miles from Greensboro, figured prominently in the early development of Greene County. Upon this favorable site was located Georgia's first paper mill, followed by Greene County's first major cotton mill.

During the War of 1812, when the supply of foreign paper dwindled to a mere trickle, two Georgia entrepreneurs named Zacharia Sims and George Paschal sought a solution to the paper shortage. They selected a site on the Oconee River, called Scull Shoals, and poured all they had into a mill to manufacture paper. In addition to producing paper, Sims and Paschal also operated an adjacent gristmill and distillery. Though flourishing for a few years, the bold enterprise ultimately failed.

Many years later, the property was purchased by Thomas Poullain, who erected Greene County's first cotton mill upon the site. To power the huge mill, Poullain built a dam across the lazy waters of the Oconee and dug a 400-foot-long millrace to carry water from the millpond to the ponderous mill wheel. Named the Scull Shoals Manufacturing Company, the mill spun crude cotton fiber into yarn, which was woven into cloth and heavy bagging for cotton bales.

When the original wooden mill building was destroyed by fire in 1845, Poullain quickly replaced it with a spacious four-story brick structure. By 1853, the prosperous mill employed nearly 500 workers and consumed over 4,000 bales of locally grown cotton per year. The severe social and economic changes which followed the close of the Civil War, however, spelled disaster for Poullain's mill. Becoming increasingly unprofitable, the struggling mill finally closed its doors in 1884.

Today, the ruins of the Scull Shoals Manufacturing Company lie within the Oconee National Forest Recreation Area. They can be reached by a leisurely 20 minute stroll along the river's east bank from the boat landing located off Georgia Highway 15.

Sope Creek Ruins

Perched among the gently rolling hills and lush ravines of eastern Cobb County sit the spectacular ruins of a large, century-old paper mill. Established in 1859, the Marietta Paper Mill channeled the impounded waters of Sope Creek into a steady stream of printing, writing, and wrapping paper. During the Civil War, the mill also supplied much of the paper on which Confederate currency and bonds were printed. When General William T. Sherman approached the enemy city of Atlanta in the summer of 1864, he ordered the paper mill destroyed; its fire-blackened walls became known as "Sherman's calling cards."

Quickly rebuilt after the war, the mill resumed operations in 1869. But the troubled economic times of the early 1870s fell heavily upon the Marietta Paper Mill. Forced into bankruptcy, the mill was sold at public auction to former Georgia Governor James Brown. Brown reorganized the company and incorporated it as the Marietta Paper Manufacturing Company the following year.

Revitalized and economically sound, the paper mill enjoyed a thriving business for many years, churning out a variety of high quality paper products from old rags, cotton stalks, and pulp wood. In 1889, a paper twine factory was added, and the following year the mill began manufacturing the first blotting paper made south of Richmond. Just a few years later, however, much of the mill's machinery was relocated to new facilities in Marietta. By 1902, the mill's operations on Sope Creek had come to a close.

Today, the rock-wall ruins lie scattered about picturesque Sope Creek, just six miles east of Marietta. Named for Old Sope, a kindly Cherokee Indian who lived nearby and told Indian stories to the neighborhood children, the creek now flows through the Sope Creek unit of the Chattahoochee River National Recreation Area. Protected by the National Park Service, the ruins beckon visitors to reach out and touch the past.

The largest ruin, that of the main building, may be reached by leaving Paper Mill Road and following an old stone reinforced path hugging the east bank for approximately one quarter mile downstream. The 300-foot-long building was divided into five rooms and stood three stories high at one point. A series of skeletal stone columns, which formerly supported the large mill sluice, lead upstream to the old dam site.

On the opposite side of the creek, the large ruin just south of Paper Mill Road was the pulp grinding facility. The 100-foot-long building once stood two stories tall. The ruins of many smaller structures, now slowly disintegrating with time, can be found along the heavily wooded banks on both sides of the creek and road.

Sunbury

The colonial town of Sunbury, situated on the Midway River 28 miles south of Savannah, figured prominently in the early history of Georgia and the United States. Three signers of the Declaration of Independence, three United States Senators, one U.S. Representative, and four Georgia Governors hailed from this tiny seaport. These men, as well as many other Sunbury citizens, helped to shape the United States and defend them from foreign rule. Today, however, this former leading port and political center is numbered among the "dead towns" of Georgia.

In 1752, a group of Puritan colonists from South Carolina migrated to Midway, Georgia. There they reaped many benefits from the land, and produced a variety of goods for export. To avoid the long overland route to the distant docks at Savannah, in 1758 the colonists established the seaport of Sunbury, just 11 miles away. Sunbury thrived, and soon rivaled Savannah in commercial importance. Ships arrived from around the globe for cargoes of locally produced rice, indigo, and lumber products. Sunbury's success was to be short-lived, however.

During the Revolutionary War, Sunbury was captured by the British. Much of the town was destroyed and subsequently abandoned, beginning a downhill journey that eventually turned Sunbury into a cemetery. While the ports of Savannah to the north and Darien to the south continued to grow and prosper throughout the 19th century, Sunbury struggled merely to survive. Malaria and other debilitating diseases took a heavy toll on the townspeople. An epidemic of yellow fever in the 1850s proved the final, fatal blow. Sunbury slipped into obscurity shortly thereafter. Today, the town has vanished, swallowed by time and earth. Only the cemetery remains, a burial ground of hopes, dreams, and expectations.

Christ Church

Nestled among the moss-laden live oaks on St. Simons Island, Christ Church stands as a testimony to one man's love for God and humanity. The quaint wooden structure with its high-spired belfry and its narrow stained-glass windows continues to serve as a devoted house of worship.

The parish of Christ Church, Frederica, was organized in 1807 and soon became the center of religious life on St. Simons. At first, the congregation gathered for worship in their homes. In 1820, a site was selected on the northern end of the island, near the town of Frederica, and a small, square church building was constructed. Upon this same site, brothers Charles and John Wesley (founders of the Methodist Church) had preached God's Word to the garrison at Fort Frederica in 1736.

The original building was nearly wrecked by Federal soldiers who occupied St. Simons during the Civil War. The altar was smashed, pews burned, windows broken out, and the organ demolished. Lacking funds to repair the damage, the parishioners were again forced to hold weekly services in their homes.

In the late 1870s, help arrived in the form of Anson Phelps Dodge. Drawn to St. Simons by his company's bountiful timber harvests, Dodge quickly fell in love with the island's people and chose to make their home his home. Dodge erected a beautiful new church building upon the site of the old house of worship, partly as a memorial to his first wife, Ellen, who had died while the young couple were honeymooning in India.

But his concern and support did not end with merely funding the church's construction. Inspired by his love for God and people, Dodge attended theological seminary and became rector of Christ Church in 1884. He devoted the remaining 14 years of his life to the Diocese of Georgia.

Dahlonega Gold Museum

For many years, the excited cries of "Thar's gold in them thar hills!" (or something to that effect) rang loud and true in the North Georgia mountains. When handsome nuggets of the precious yellow metal were first discovered in 1828, prospectors flocked to the hills, setting in motion the nation's first gold rush. Soon studded with mining camps and boom towns, the North Georgia mountains quickly yielded up their treasure.

With pans and sluice boxes, the miners carefully worked the streams, picking out the many bits of gold washed down from rich mother lodes located high up in the mountains. As these placer deposits began drying up, the miners turned their attention to the mountains themselves. Using picks, shovels, and gunpowder (dynamite would not be invented for another 40 years), the miners bore deep into the mountains, removing huge quantities of ore. The ore was sent to nearby stamp mills where it was crushed nearly to a powder and the valuable metal was extracted.

At first, much of the gold was shipped to Philadelphia where it was fashioned into coins at the United States mint. In 1838, however, the Federal government opened a branch mint in Dahlonega. Over the next twenty years, the mint stamped out nearly 1-1/2 million gold coins worth more than $6 million. (With the outbreak of civil war, the mint closed in 1861. The building was destroyed by fire 17 years later.)

By the late 1840s the gold had largely played out. Although a few mines continued to operate well into the 20th century, the glory days of Georgia's gold rush had drawn to a close. In 1849, when gold fever struck again, this time in California, many of Georgia's miners hurried west in search of their fortunes. But the story of Georgia's early miners and their quest for gold lives on in the Dahlonega Gold Museum, housed in the former Lumpkin County Courthouse.

Designated the county seat in 1833, Dahlonega (from the Cherokee word "dalanigei" meaning gold) was one boom town that did not go bust. Built in 1836, the courthouse served a variety of needs. The first floor functioned as a marketplace, while the courtroom, judges' chambers, and county offices were located upstairs. When a new courthouse was erected in 1965, the old building was presented to the State of Georgia for use as a museum. Like the surrounding hills, the museum's brick walls and the mortar binding them together reveal traces of gold.

There is still gold in the North Georgia mountains, though now it is much more difficult to find. But who knows? Maybe the richest lode of all still awaits discovery.

Stone Mountain's Confederate Memorial Carving

Bulging from the ground 16 miles east of Atlanta, Stone Mountain is the world's largest lump of exposed granite. Etched on the face of this monolithic mass is the world's biggest carving, a lasting memorial to the Confederacy which struggled so desperately to preserve the Southern way of life.

Stone Mountain was formed eons ago when molten rock from deep within the earth forced its way upward, nearly to the planet's surface. As the rock cooled over time, the material above was slowly eroded away, eventually exposing the huge mass. Today the mountain protrudes 825 feet above the surrounding countryside, but much more of the rock still lies below the surface.

In 1838 entrepreneur Aaron Cloud erected a simple wooden tower on the mountain's summit. For fifty cents a visitor could climb the 165-foot-tall tower for a bird's eye view of the mountain and surrounding countryside. Stone Mountain had become one of the state's earliest tourist attractions.

But tourism soon gave way to trade. With the coming of the railroad in the mid-1840s, Stone Mountain granite became a commercially viable commodity, and quarries quickly sprang up on the mountain's flanks. For years the quarries flourished, as workers chiseled out paving blocks for city streets and building blocks for countless banks, post offices, courthouses, and other structures built throughout the world. Two of the quarrymen, William Venable and his brother Samuel, continually expanded their operations until they had acquired the entire mountain.

When members of the United Daughters of the Confederacy approached the Venables for permission to use Stone Mountain as the site for an enormous confederate memorial, the families graciously deeded the north face of the mountain and ten adjoining acres to the organization. The deed stipulated, however, that the carving must be completed within 12 years or the land would revert to the original owners. A managing association was formed to carry the project forward on a formal basis, and renowned sculptor Gutzon Borglum was commissioned for the carving. Borglum's ambitious design called for seven central figures accompanied by "an army of thousands."

Funding problems and manpower requirements for World War I delayed the project's start for nearly seven years. Finally, amid much fanfare on June 23, 1923, Borglum at last began work on the carving. But differences of opinion soon arose between the sculptor and members of the managing association. When these disagreements grew to irreconcilable proportions in 1925, Borglum packed his tools, abandoned his work, and left for South Dakota. There he gained lasting fame by chiseling the heads of four presidents into the resilient rock of Mount Rushmore. The carving at Stone Mountain fell into the capable hands of sculptor Augustus Lukeman.

Lukeman blasted away Borglum's unfinished carving and began work on a new, simpler design featuring three prominent figures mounted on horseback. Racing against time, the sculptor hurried to complete the carving by the deadline. But the work proved too hard and the remaining time too little. With the carving far from finished, the Venables reclaimed their property on May 20, 1928. For many years, the only carving which took place on the mountain occurred in the quarries.

In 1958, the State of Georgia purchased the mountain and the surrounding land and created the Stone Mountain Memorial Association to administer the property. The granite quarries were closed down and the mountain was slowly transformed into one of Georgia's premiere tourist attractions. In 1963, sculptor Walker Hancock was chosen to finish Lukeman's carving.

Since the earlier years when first Borglum then Lukeman had pounded away at the hard granite with chisels and pneumatic drills, a powerful new rock-cutting technique had been developed. Called the thermo-jet torch, the tool's high temperature flame could easily slice through the tough rock. Even so, chief carver Roy Faulkner and his assistants labored on the mountain's face for six years to complete the carving. The long-awaited dedication ceremony for Stone Mountain's Confederate Memorial Carving finally took place on May 9, 1970.

Today, the figures of three Civil War heroes, Confederate President Jefferson Davis, General Robert E. Lee, and General Thomas J. "Stonewall" Jackson appear to ride from the face of the mountain. The carving, measuring 90 by 190 feet, is recessed more than 40 feet into the mountain, in a frame larger than a football field. Of truly enormous proportions, the carving is a lasting tribute indeed.

Porterdale Mills

In 1868, Colonel E. Steadman purchased a huge tract of land
on the Yellow River, where he established the township of Steadman, and erected a mill to manufacture both cotton and woolen
fabrics. Steadman later sold the property to O.S. Porter, who
renamed the town Porterdale and the factory Porterdale Mills.

Located three miles southwest of Covington in Newton
County, Porterdale Mills was the world's largest manufacturer
of cotton rope, supplying most of the rope used by the U.S. Navy
during World War II. The mill throbbed with the activity of nearly 3,000 workers toiling 24 hours a day, seven days a week.

Then, in the 1960s, the tenuous thread of life unraveled for
Porterdale Mills when the plant suddenly closed for economic
reasons. Today, the buildings appear dark and desolate, the machinery lying in muted silence, its era of work drawn to a close.

Chapter 8:

There's No Place Like Home

1 Little White House
2 Liberty Hall
3 Oak Hill
4 Wormslow
5 Horton House

6 Jarrell Plantation
7 Hay House
8 Rhodes Hall
9 Herndon Home
10 Travelers Rest

Little White House

Tucked into the woods on the north slope of Pine Mountain, near the town of Warm Springs, the Little White House was the Georgia home of President Franklin Delano Roosevelt. In this little house the President spent many of his happiest days, fashioning new ideas that influenced thinking around the world. With wisdom and foresight, Roosevelt led the nation to economic recovery following the Great Depression, and through the difficult years of World War II. He was the only President to be elected to four terms of office. Now preserved as a state historic site, Roosevelt's Little White House appears much as it did on the afternoon of April 12, 1945, when the President died in his bedroom, the victim of a fatal stroke.

Roosevelt first came to Warm Springs in 1924, seeking a cure for the infantile paralysis (polio) which had struck him three years before. Although the warm, mineral-rich water held no miraculous cure, it did bring improvement. During his many visits over the next few years, Roosevelt gained strength in both body and mind, and became charmed with the rolling countryside and its friendly people. He decided to make his home there.

The Little White House was completed in 1932, while Roosevelt was still governor of his native New York. A small guest house was added in 1933, after he became President. Roosevelt's home was unpretentious; the six modestly furnished rooms reflect the President's preference for simple living.

As President, Roosevelt immediately faced a huge challenge. The United States had slipped into the midst of a great depression. The nation's economy was almost paralyzed with many thousands of workers jobless. Banks were closing by the hundreds. Quick to act, Roosevelt offered Americans a New Deal. The policies and programs implemented under his presidency, such as the National Bank Holiday, the Civilian Conservation Corps, and the Rural Electrification Administration, laid the foundation for a return to national prosperity. The President's expert leadership was equally important in guiding the nation through the dark years of World War II.

On the afternoon of April 12, 1945, while posing for a portrait in his living room, Roosevelt suffered a massive cerebral hemorrhage. The President was gently carried to his bedroom, where he died at 3:35 PM. Like the Little White House, the unfinished portrait remains where it was, as it was, when one of America's greatest leaders passed into history.

Liberty Hall

Liberty Hall was the home of Alexander Hamilton Stephens, one of the Old South's most remarkable politicians. Born on a small farm just north of Crawfordville in 1812, Stephens became a talented lawyer, a dedicated statesman, and the unsullied vice president of the Confederacy.

Frail and sickly most of his adult life, Stephens nevertheless delivered fiery orations before his fellow politicians in Washington. Throughout the 1840s and 1850s, as Congress fought over issues which would eventually lead to war, Stephens arose on numerous occasions to lend forceful support for measures intended to preserve the Union. Stephens was openly opposed to secession. However, when Georgia delegates voted overwhelmingly to secede in 1861, Stephens joined his constituency in creating the Confederate States of America. He was elected vice president of the ill-fated Confederacy later that same year.

Throughout the ensuing civil war, Stephens battled bitterly with President Jefferson Davis. Stephens perceived Davis as a dictator who was aiming for absolute power, and vehemently opposed Davis' "total war measures" which severely restricted the rights of the individual. Unfortunately, the great rift which developed between these two high-ranking officials did little to unite the Southern cause.

With the fall of the Confederacy in 1865, Stephens' illustrious political career came to a temporary end. On May 11, 1865, he was arrested by Federal troops and sent to prison. When released five months later, Stephens returned to Liberty Hall. There he found that, despite the war, life had changed very little. As a slaveholder, Stephens had been a gentle and fair master. Consequently, many of his former slaves remained with him as paid servants during the post-war years.

In 1872 Stephens returned to Congress. But, crippled by an accident three years earlier and afflicted with various maladies, he rarely spoke out as he had in the past. In 1882 Stephens was elected governor of Georgia. He died four months after taking office.

Stephens had purchased Liberty Hall in 1845. The modest, wood-framed house formed the center of a medium-sized plantation on the outskirts of Crawfordville. In 1858 Stephens added the rear veranda and the unique library/bedroom wing. In 1875 he had the main house torn down and rebuilt, using the old building materials wherever possible. Liberty Hall became a state historic site in 1932.

Oak Hill

Built in 1847 on a gentle knoll just north of Rome, Oak Hill was the childhood home of Martha Berry, one of Georgia's foremost educators. Although Oak Hill is a striking example of a classic Southern plantation home, Martha Berry was not a traditional Southern woman. Against formidable odds, she fought to provide a quality education for the mountain children of Northwest Georgia. The unique institution she founded in 1902 has grown into today's thriving Berry College.

Born on October 7, 1866, Martha Berry was the second oldest of eight children. As a child, Martha was greatly influenced by her father's unwavering concern for the welfare of others and his wonderful generosity. She often accompanied him on his many missions of mercy, offering assistance to families struggling through the dark years following the Civil War. Martha eventually found her own destiny in meeting the needs of her neighbors. Hers was a life of self-sacrifice, determination, and devotion.

Martha donated the money and land her father had given her, and committed herself to the task of educating the young highlanders. What began as a small Sunday School in a log-cabin playhouse at Oak Hill soon grew into a boys' boarding school. Under Martha's careful supervision, the students received an education of the mind, the heart, and the hands.

To help pay their expenses, the boys worked for the school at a variety of jobs. They planted crops, ran a dairy, and built many of the school buildings. They gathered their own stones, milled their own lumber, and made their own brick. As they worked, they acquired many new skills that would help them live more productive lives in the mountains.

Over the years, the institution continued to grow. A Girls' School was added in 1909. A junior college was begun in 1926, which became a full-fledged four-year college a few years later. The college grew in size as well as stature. Today, the Berry College campus stretches across 28,000 acres.

Martha Berry died on February 27, 1942, but her legacy lives on in the students, faculty, and alumni of Berry College.

Wormslow

Seven miles southeast of Savannah, on the southern tip of a peninsula named the "Isle of Hope" stand the ruins of one of Georgia's first colonial estates. Rich in history, the crumbling tabby walls are all that remain of a fortified house built between 1739 and 1745 by one of Georgia's first English settlers to protect his family from a feared Spanish attack. That man was Noble Jones, and he called his home "Wormslow."

Jones and his family were among the 114 colonists who sailed to Savannah with James Edward Oglethorpe aboard the ship *Anne* in 1733. Because slavery was not initially allowed in the newly found colony of Georgia, Jones brought with him two indentured servants, 17-year-old Thomas Ellis and 11-year-old Mary Cormock. After living in Savannah for three years, Jones received a sizable land grant of 500 acres.

In England, Jones had been a physician and carpenter, skills that served him well in the New World. After erecting a crude residence on his new land, Jones painstakingly cleared 20 acres of forest and planted corn, beans, and a variety of other food crops. Although the poor soil made farming difficult, Jones also grew cotton, indigo, and a few other cash crops. Day after day, Jones and his family toiled alongside servants Thomas and Mary in the fields.

In the late 1730s, tensions mounted between Spain and England as the two rivals vied for control of the colonial coast and inland territories. After Oglethorpe unsuccessfully laid siege to the Spanish stronghold of St. Augustine, he feared a retaliatory invasion of Georgia. To defend Savannah against an attack from the south, Oglethorpe stationed a company of "marines" at Wormslow, which was strategically located on part of an inland water approach to that city. The men were placed under the command of Noble Jones.

To further safeguard his family and servants, Jones decided to build a new residence out of a strong coastal concrete called tabby. Building the unique, fortified house proved a major undertaking, and Jones enlisted the help of the soldiers who had been placed under his command. Nearly six years went into the home's construction, along with thousands of bushels of sand, shell, and lime.

When completed, the five-room house stood 1-1/2 stories tall and was surrounded by thick tabby walls standing eight feet high. The walls created a rectangular fort which was 80 feet long and 70 feet wide. Bastions located at the four corners provided a flanking fire which effectively covered all approaches. Within his sturdy domicile Jones at last felt safe and secure, but the feared Spanish attack never came.

Noble Jones died in 1775, on the eve of the American Revolution. The land remained in the hands of his descendants until acquired by the State of Georgia two centuries later. Today, the tabby ruins of Wormslow are a treasured state historic site.

Horton House

Swept by the ceaseless tides of the Atlantic Ocean, Jekyll Island is a narrow strip of sand just nine miles long by little more than a mile wide. Southernmost of Georgia's Golden Isles, the island was named by Georgia's founder, James Edward Oglethorpe, to honor his friend and benefactor Sir Joseph Jekyll. At the north end of the island stands a two-story ruin, the former residence of Major William Horton. Built in 1742, the ruin is one of Georgia's oldest standing tabby structures.

The 18-inch thick walls of the Horton House have weathered two and a half centuries of sun, sea, and storm surprisingly well.

Like many other colonial buildings, the Horton House was made from tabby, a special blend of sand, lime, and oyster shells mixed with water and poured into forms to harden. This quick and convenient building technique was brought to the New World by the Spaniards. A thin coating of plaster applied to the walls prevented the razor-sharp edges of protruding shells from tearing clothes and flesh.

Major Horton, one of Oglethorpe's most trusted officers, became the first Englishman to settle on Jekyll Island. There he established a large plantation, cultivating crops to supply settlers at Frederica on nearby St. Simons Island. Horton also grew barley, rye, and hops, the necessary ingredients for beer, which he fermented and sold to soldiers stationed at Fort Frederica. The tabby remains of Georgia's first brewery lie along a small creek just southwest of Horton's house.

In the early 1790s, Jekyll Island was purchased by Poulain du Bignon, a much-decorated French naval captain whose loyalty to Louis XVI during the French Revolution forced him to flee his beloved homeland. Du Bignon moved his family into the old tabby house on the Horton plantation, where he eventually made a fortune growing fine Sea Island Cotton.

For nearly a century, the du Bignon dynasty ruled over Jekyll. Then, in 1886, the island was sold to some of America's wealthiest men, who formed the famous Jekyll Island Club. For over 50 years, members of the exclusive club relaxed and entertained on their own private isle. In 1947, the State of Georgia bought Jekyll Island from the club for use as a state park, and today it may be visited and enjoyed by all.

Jarrell Plantation

In the 1840s, John Fitz Jarrell built the first dwelling on the land now occupied by the historic Jarrell Plantation. For the next century and a half, he and his descendents worked the soil, successfully living off the land. Through resourcefulness and old-fashioned country ingenuity, the family overcame the ravages of war and the hardships of economic depression. The work was hard, but the reward was equal to the task. Theirs is a legacy of living in harmony with nature.

Situated on gently rolling hills a dozen miles north of Macon, Jarrell Plantation effectively compresses 150 years of Georgia agricultural history into just a few acres. The family's original dwelling still stands, as do many other buildings housing the tools and equipment which formed an important part of their everyday life.

Jarrell Plantation was a typical middle Georgia estate, though vastly different from the idealized modern stereotype. Missing was the grand plantation mansion with tall columns and wide verandas. In its place was a plain, four-room home built from rough, hand-sawn lumber. Plantation architecture, from homes to barns to workshops, emphasized functionality in simple wooden structures.

In the heyday of cotton production before the Civil War, cotton fields stretched across the plantation's 600 acres. During the war, however, emphasis shifted from growing this cash crop to the more essential production of foodstuffs. After the war, diversification became the key as Southern plantations attempted to regain some measure of their antebellum prosperity. Besides growing a variety of crops, including corn, wheat, and sugar cane, the Jarrell family obtained additional income by ginning, threshing, and milling for their neighbors, as well as performing occasional lumbering operations.

Now part of a rapidly vanishing culture, the old syrup mill, cotton gin, gristmill, sawmill, blacksmith shop, and carpenter shop form just a few of the 20 historic buildings preserved at Jarrell Plantation. They housed the essential tools of the trade, used by successful farmers not only in Jones County of middle Georgia, but by successful farmers throughout the United States. A visit to Jarrell Plantation is a journey back in time, to an era when family farms provided all the basic necessities of life for those who chose to live upon the land.

Hay House

When built in the 1850s, Hay House may have been the most advanced antebellum house in America. Located at 934 Georgia Avenue, this magnificent Macon mansion sported an elevator, indoor hot and cold plumbing, a room-to-room intercom, and the most sophisticated ventilation system of its time. In addition, the detailed plasterwork, marbleized walls, and frescoed ceilings of this architectural masterpiece bespeak the beauty and grandeur of a time now past.

Architect Griffith Thomas used the finest materials and innovative building techniques to create Hay House, a major project requiring five years to complete. From the stately dining room with its deep paneling of solid walnut and stained glass windows, to the palatial ballroom and luxurious drawing room lit by elegant crystal chandeliers, this was Southern comfort at its best. In fact, before its light was forever dimmed by the Civil War, Hay House was, itself, a symbol of Southern hospitality.

Originally built for Macon entrepreneur William Butler Johnston, the house was purchased by Parker Lee Hay in 1926. The Hay family lived in the house until 1977. Today, the house is owned by the Georgia Trust for Historic Preservation. But the house's 24 rooms, encompassing some 18,000 square feet of living space, are still filled with the fine furnishings and splendid works of art collected by the Hay family from all over the world.

Rhodes Hall

Dwarfed by high-rises and nearly smothered in traffic, the magnificent stone mansion at 1516 Peachtree Street in downtown Atlanta was the home of Amos and Amanda Rhodes. Better known as Rhodes Hall, the house harks back to an earlier era, when this portion of Peachtree was a fashionable suburban neighborhood.

Born in Kentucky in 1850, Amos Giles Rhodes moved to Atlanta when he was 24 years old. In the late 1870s, Rhodes opened a small store where he sold medium-priced furniture on credit. An immediate success, Rhodes Furniture grew into one of the country's largest chains of furniture stores. By the turn of the century, Rhodes had become one of Atlanta's wealthiest businessmen.

Construction of Rhodes Hall began in 1902, and was completed two years later. Built of Stone Mountain granite, the mansion was patterned after the beautiful Rhineland castles Rhodes had once admired on a trip to Europe. The three-story house is as richly ornamented on the inside as it is solid on the outside. From the hardwood parquet floors and fine mahogany woodwork, to the elaborately decorated plaster ceilings, Rhodes spared no cost in the construction of his home.

One of the house's most unique features is a beautiful series of painted and stained glass windows set in the wall above the curved staircase leading to the second floor. Created by the Von Gerichten Art Glass Company, the windows depict the rise and fall of the Confederacy. The three panels, consisting of over 1,250 pieces of glass, chronicle the Confederacy from Jefferson Davis' inauguration as President to Robert E. Lee's surrender at Appomattox.

The Rhodes estate originally included over 125 acres and encompassed most of the present-day Brookwood interchange of Interstates 75 and 85. Engulfed by Atlanta's growing metropolitan area, today the estate covers less than an acre.

A year after Rhodes died in 1928, his family donated the mansion to the State of Georgia. It is now operated as a house museum by the Georgia Trust for Historic Preservation.

Herndon Home

Located in the historic district of Atlanta University, the Herndon Home chronicles the "rags to riches" story of Alonzo Herndon, a former slave who became one of America's most prominent Black businessmen.

Alonzo Franklin Herndon was born a slave in Walton County on June 26, 1858. Freed by the Civil War, Herndon worked as a farm hand and sharecropper. He learned to cut hair at the age of 20, and soon moved to Atlanta, where his fame and fortune began.

Although he lacked a formal education, Herndon had a flair for business. He eventually owned three barbershops in Atlanta. One barbershop, located at 66 Peachtree Street, was considered the most elegant in the country. The shop featured bronze and crystal chandeliers, marble floors and walls, and porcelain barber chairs. Herndon's barbershops marked the beginning of a highly successful business career.

On October 31, 1893, Alonzo married Adrienne McNeil, a drama instructor at Atlanta University. The couple's only child, a son named Norris, was born on July 15, 1897. Adrienne died from Addison's disease on April 6, 1910. Two years later, Alonzo remarried. He and Jessie (Gillespie) Herndon had no children.

Alonzo and his first wife, Adrienne, designed the Herndon Home in 1908, without the aid of an architect. The 6,000-square-foot, two-story brick structure was built almost entirely by Black craftsmen. The historic house, which boasts beveled glass windows, mahogany paneling, and parquet flooring, is as impressive today as when it was completed in 1912.

Herndon's most significant business venture was the founding of the Atlanta Life Insurance Company in 1905. The company not only provided affordable insurance to low-income Black families, it also offered mortgages to Blacks who were often denied financing by banks. From humble beginnings, Atlanta Life grew into one of the largest Black insurance companies in the country.

When Alonzo died in 1927, his son, Norris, became president of Atlanta Life. Alonzo's second wife, Jessie, became vice president, a position she held until her death in 1947. Following in his father's footsteps, Norris led the company to its period of greatest growth and prosperity.

Norris also continued his father's tradition of philanthropy. In 1933, he and Jessie gave the Herndon Barbershop at 66 Peachtree Street to its employees. When Jessie died in 1947, Norris gave $500,000 to Morris Brown College for the construction of a stadium. He also donated money to numerous churches and civic organizations. In 1950, Norris formed the Herndon Foundation to carry on the family's spirit of giving.

Norris never married. When he died in 1977, he left the family home and its contents, including his eclectic art collection, to the charitable foundation he had established. Today, the Herndon Home remains a lasting tribute to the extraordinary talent and generosity of a remarkable family.

Travelers Rest

Located six miles east of Toccoa in northeast Georgia, Travelers Rest was the 19th century home of Devereaux Jarrett. Known as "the richest man in the Tugaloo Valley," Jarrett owned a huge plantation along a dusty frontier road called the Unicoi Turnpike. In the mid-1830s Jarrett enlarged his house and opened it as an inn to weary turnpike travelers.

Jarrett and his family lived on the first floor of the rustic, clapboard-sided structure. Guest rooms and a small post office were located upstairs. Family and guests ate together in a large dining room on the main floor. To reduce heat and lessen the risk of fire, food was cooked in a detached kitchen. Separate family and guest parlors were also located on the main floor.

Travelers Rest offered food and shelter to wayfarers until shortly after the Civil War. In 1955 the house was purchased by the state and is now operated as a state historic site.

Chapter 9:

In Defense
of the Land

1 Fort King George
2 Fort Frederica
3 Fort Morris
4 Fort Jackson

5 Fort McAllister
6 Fort Pulaski
7 Fort Yargo

Fort King George

In the spring of 1721, threatened with French expansionism in the New World, the British erected a small fort on a bluff overlooking the Altamaha River in what is now coastal Georgia. Garrisoned by British soldiers from His Majesty's 41st Independent Company, Fort King George became the southernmost outpost of the British Empire in North America. Not for another 12 years would this land be included in the King's charter to James Edward Oglethorpe for the last of the original thirteen colonies — Georgia.

The work of constructing the fort was carried out by men from the colony of South Carolina under the direction of Colonel John "Tuscarora Jack" Barnwell. In addition to a simple but sturdy cypress blockhouse, the fort included officers' quarters, barracks, and several smaller structures surrounded by a moat and a palisade. Though built to deter the French, the fort's garrison was withdrawn to Port Royal just six years after the fort was completed, when another world power, Spain, threatened the outlying plantations of the Carolina Colony. Abandoned, the fort soon fell into ruin.

Today, an authentically reconstructed blockhouse dominates this historic site, which is administered by the Georgia Department of Natural Resources. The remains of three large sawmills also pepper the site, which once formed part of the timber capital of the Southeast. As early as 1736, crude pit saws were set up in this location to convert trees into lumber for the rapidly growing towns of Savannah, Frederica, and Darien.

With vast stands of live oak and longleaf pine, both essential materials for ship-building, the area around Fort King George enjoyed a sawmilling boom which lasted nearly 200 years. The nearby town of Darien, located on the mouth of the Altamaha, became one of the world's largest timber exporters. When the big trees finally played out, however, the timber industry reluctantly moved on, leaving behind its ghostly reminders for future generations.

Fort Frederica National Monument

In 1733, James Edward Oglethorpe established the last of the thirteen original colonies on the coast of the New World. The colony, called Georgia in honor of Britain's King George II, lay just below South Carolina, dangerously close to Spanish-owned Florida.

To protect his fledgling settlements from Spanish attack, Oglethorpe built a strong defensive outpost atop a small bluff on the west side of St. Simons Island. Finished in 1736, the outpost was called Fort Frederica in honor of Frederick, Prince of Wales, King George's son. A town, also called Frederica, sprang up alongside the fort.

The colonists employed tabby construction extensively throughout the fort and town. Similar to concrete, tabby consisted of sand, lime, and oyster shell mixed with water and poured into forms. To obtain the necessary lime, Oglethorpe's settlers burned oyster shells gathered from ancient Indian shell mounds.

When the Spaniards invaded Georgia in July of 1742, they focused their attack on Fort Frederica, the "Gibraltar of North America." If the vital fort fell, the door to both Georgia and South Carolina would open wide. But Oglethorpe's infantry put up a rigid defense, soundly defeating the Spanish at the Battle of Bloody Marsh on July 7. As a result, Spain quietly recalled its soldiers, ending forever the threat of Spanish domination of Georgia.

No longer needed, Oglethorpe's famous regiment was disbanded a few years later and the fort was abandoned. Largely dependent upon the military for its livelihood, the once-thriving community of Frederica soon became one of Georgia's first ghost towns. In 1945, the crumbling ruins of town and fort, lodged among magnificent live oak heavily draped with Spanish moss, were officially preserved as a National Monument.

Fort Morris

Erected in 1776, Fort Morris was a fairly substantial earthwork situated on a low bluff above the Midway River, less than a quarter mile from the once-thriving seaport of Sunbury. In addition to defending this colonial town during the Revolutionary War, the fort also served as a base for three unsuccessful expeditions against British forces in Florida.

Fort Morris was irregularly shaped, having four sides varying in length from 140 to 275 feet. An earthen parapet surrounded a parade of about an acre in size; at the center of which stood a large brick barracks. Armed with two dozen pieces of artillery, the fort was designed to repel attacks from both land and sea.

On November 25, 1778, British Colonel L.V. Fuser landed at nearby Sunbury, captured the town, and promptly demanded the fort's surrender. Although he had less than 200 men pitted against Fuser's 500 seasoned troops and their fully armed warships, Colonel John McIntosh defiantly replied, "Come and take it!" Fuser declined the offer and the British temporarily withdrew from Sunbury.

In January of 1779, the British returned. Commanding an overwhelming British force, General Augustin Prevost demanded the immediate and unconditional surrender of the fort. When Major Joseph Lane, then in command of the fort's garrison, refused, British cannons began hammering away at the fort. After a brief but intense bombardment, Fort Morris fell to the British, who thereafter used it as a prison for American officers.

When the British finally abandoned Georgia in 1782, the once-bustling seaport of Sunbury was in ruins, much of it intentionally burned to the ground. During the War of 1812, when the British again sought dominion over the New World, the remains of Fort Morris were recast into a more compact defensive structure called Fort Defiance. The hard-packed earthworks are now part of the Fort Morris Historic Site administered by the Georgia Department of Natural Resources.

Fort Jackson

At the beginning of the 19th century, the United States clung tenuously to its freshly won freedom. Threatened by powerful adversaries across the ocean, in 1808 President Thomas Jefferson called for the construction of a number of forts to strengthen America's coast. As part of this new coastal defense system, two fortifications were placed to protect the important harbor at Savannah. One of these brick bastions, Fort Pulaski, was erected on nearby Cockspur Island. The other fort — named for James Jackson, a hero of the Revolutionary War and past governor of Georgia — was built within sight of the city itself.

With construction barely begun, Fort Jackson consisted of little more than a brick battery, crude wooden barracks, and a

126

wooden palisade when war erupted with Great Brittain in 1812. Nevertheless, a garrison of U.S. Infantry and Savannah militia manned the fort for the duration of the war. After the war, a deep moat was dug, brick barracks were built, and the rear wall and sally port were added.

In 1861, when hostilities between North and South mushroomed into civil war, the Georgia militia seized both Fort Pulaski and Fort Jackson. Edward Anderson, former mayor of Savannah, assumed command at Jackson. Anderson had a garrison of 150 men and nine cannons with which to repel the Union navy.

Unlike Pulaski, which could be avoided by sailing up the Wilmington River from the south or around Daufuskie Island from the north, Fort Jackson was strategically situated on the ship channel immediately below the city. Any vessel, friend or foe, bound for the harbor had to pass this venerable defensive work.

Indeed, when Fort Pulaski fell in April of 1862, Fort Jackson and the outlying earthen batteries became the key to Savannah's river defense. For nearly three more years, Fort Jackson's men and guns held the Federal fleet at bay. When the Confederates were eventually forced to evacuate Savannah in December of 1864, the cause was not threat by sea, but by land. Marching virtually unopposed, Union General William T. Sherman and his invasionary force had arrived from Atlanta.

Following the Civil War, Fort Jackson underwent additional modifications, but its days were numbered. The inherent vulnerability of brick and mortar to modern rifled artillery — so graphically demonstrated by the breaching of Pulaski and the utter destruction of Fort Sumter at Charleston, South Carolina — brought the era of massive masonry fortifications to a close. The fort was finally abandoned in 1905. Today, the eight-acre site, appearing much as it did during the 1860s, is managed by the Coastal Heritage Society.

Fort McAllister

A few miles down the coast from Savannah, just below Seven Mile Bend on the Ogeechee River, lies the Confederate stronghold of Fort McAllister. This massive earthwork, nestled against the river's south bank, was hastily erected in 1861 to keep Union vessels out of the important Ogeechee waterway.

Unlike nearby Fort Pulaski, whose masonry walls quickly crumbled under a barrage of rifled artillery fire in April, 1862, the earthen mounds of McAllister proved virtually impenetrable to all that the Union navy could bring against them. Though pummeled with shot and shell, the fort repeatedly withstood Federal attempts to silence it in both 1862 and 1863. The craters and furrows created in the sandy soil by impacting projectiles were easily repaired with shovels and rakes.

On March 3, 1863, the Federal navy made one last grand attempt to reduce McAllister. Three monitor-class ironclads, three wooden gunboats, and three mortar schooners dropped anchor in the Ogeechee and began blasting away at the fort. The fort responded with plunging mortar fire, red-hot shot, and exploding shell, while sharpshooters aimed their sights at distant figures occasionally visible in the open gun ports. After shelling the fort for seven grueling hours with no apparent damage, the Federals finally accepted the futility of such attempts, and henceforward saved their ammunition.

The following year and a half passed relatively quietly for the fort's garrison. Then, late in 1864 a number of Federal supply vessels suddenly appeared off the coast not far from the Ogeechee River, an ominous sign that General William T. Sherman and his army of 60,000 men were fast approaching. In anticipation, the men of McAllister dug in a little deeper.

Late in the afternoon on December 13, 1864, as General Sherman watched from across the river, Federal soldiers stormed the fort. Furious hand-to-hand combat ensued. Grossly outnumbered, the fort's garrison of 230 men, commanded by Major George W. Anderson, was soon overpowered and the fort finally subdued. The Union army had succeeded where the navy had failed.

With the fall of Fort McAllister came the fall of Savannah a few days later. Sherman's march to the sea had finally ended. In this part of Dixie, the war was over.

Fort Pulaski
National Monument

Located on little Cockspur Island, within sight of the Atlantic Ocean, Fort Pulaski stands silent guard over the river entrance to the commerce capital of Savannah. An immense monument of early 19th century brickwork, Fort Pulaski was built to shore up the deplorably weak system of coastal defenses which had nearly sealed American fate during the War of 1812. The fort was named for Count Casimir Pulaski, a Polish soldier who fell mortally wounded while rallying French and American forces at the battle of Savannah during another conflict, the American Revolution.

Nearly one million dollars and more than 25 million bricks, purchased from as far away as Baltimore, Maryland, went into the fort's construction. Blocks of granite came from New York State while huge slabs of sandstone arrived from the Connecticut River Valley. Begun in 1829, the enormous construction project required 18 years to complete.

To support the citadel's monstrous weight, wooden pilings up to 75 feet long were first driven deep into the soft mud of Cockspur. Next, a sturdy grillage of yellow pine timbers was laid across the top of the piles. Finally, the massive brick foundation was prepared and the walls erected. Over seven feet thick, the fort's solid brick ramparts were considered impregnable.

For 13 years, Fort Pulaski stood alone and lifeless, awaiting its call to protect the United States from some foreign aggressor. But, as the year 1860 drew anxiously to a close, and tensions continued to rise between North and South, the fort would soon be used to fight the divided states instead.

On January 3, 1861, just two weeks after South Carolina seceded from the Union, Georgia Governor Joseph Brown ordered the State militia to occupy Fort Pulaski. When Georgia withdrew from the Union on January 19, 1861, the fort was officially transferred to the Confederate States of America, and Colonel Charles H. Olmstead was placed in command of the fort's garrison of 385 men.

Ten months later, the Federals overran Confederate fortifications at Port Royal Sound, South Carolina, about 15 miles north of Pulaski. There they established a strong base for further operations against Confederate positions along the South Atlantic coast. Lacking sufficient troops to fully defend the many small batteries and forts peppered across the seacoast islands, and believing Fort Pulaski invulnerable to attack, the Confederates abandoned their weak fortifications on nearby Tybee Island. Unopposed, the Federals quickly swarmed over the island.

With a bold plan to reduce Fort Pulaski to rubble, Captain Quincy A. Gillmore assumed command of all Federal forces on Tybee Island in February of 1862. Over the next two months, Gillmore's men erected 11 batteries, containing 36 cannons and mortars, along the northwest shore of Tybee more than a mile from the fort. Although this distance was twice the effective range for conventional heavy ordnance, Gillmore's armament included ten new experimental weapons of warfare, rifled cannons. On the morning of April 10, 1862, the Federals opened fire.

Gillmore's rifled cannons soon demonstrated their awesome destructiveness, irresistibly drilling into the masonry walls with devastating effect. By noon of the following day, the bombardment had created a lethal, 30-foot breach in the fort's southeast angle. Explosive shells, passing through the gap and slamming into the walls of the north magazine, threatened to annihilate the fort's garrison with their own gunpowder. Consequently, Colonel Olmstead was forced to surrender the fort just 30 hours after the historic bombardment had begun.

The Federals occupied Fort Pulaski for the duration of the war. By effectively blocking the main entrance to Savannah, Pulaski added yet another stranglehold on the economic life of the South.

Many years later, on October 15, 1924, the fort was proclaimed a National Monument by President Calvin Coolidge. Today, the old fort serves not only as a memorial to humanity's courage and dedication, but also as a testimonial to the ultimate frailty of its creations.

Fort Yargo

Historic Fort Yargo is one of four 18th century wooden blockhouses built to protect early Georgia settlers from the feared Creek and Cherokee Indians. Erected in 1792, the small, two-story structure was fashioned from hefty, hand-hewn logs tightly fitted together with interlocking corners and stout wooden pegs. The large stockade that once surrounded the blockhouse has long since crumbled back into the colorful dirt of Barrow County. In 1954, the nearly 200-year-old fort was formally set aside as one of Georgia's state parks.

Chapter 10:

Lest
We
Forget

1 Chickamauga Battlefield
2 Kennesaw Battlefield
3 Pickett's Mill Battlefield

4 Andersonville Prison
5 Double-Barrelled Cannon

Chickamauga Battlefield

Created as our country's first national military park, the fields and hills of Chickamauga appear little changed from the fateful days in September of 1863 when North and South battled in some of the fiercest fighting of the Civil War. As autumn hovered over the mountains around Chattanooga, Tennessee, more than 66,000 men dressed in gray confronted nearly 60,000 men dressed in blue. Many of these brave men would not live to see the spring. Studded with hundreds of monuments and historical markers, Chickamauga Battlefield recalls the terrible strife which once enveloped our nation as brother sought to annihilate brother.

The fighting began early on the morning of September 19, when Union infantry under General William S. Rosecrans stumbled upon segments of General Braxton Bragg's Confederate cavalry just west of Chickamauga Creek. The ensuing battle leapt along a line which stretched south for nearly four miles. Desperate fighting, often hand-to-hand, continued throughout the day as the Federals were slowly but relentlessly pushed back to LaFayette Road (now US 27).

The following day, the battle erupted anew as General Bragg again attempted to break the Union line. Shortly before noon, General James Longstreet and his hard-fighting veterans from the Army of Northern Virginia punched a hole through the Union defenses. As a torrent of Confederate soldiers poured through the widening gap, General Rosecrans and nearly half his army fled the field and rushed toward Chattanooga, eight miles away. General George H. Thomas quickly took command of the remaining Federal forces and hastily formed a new battleline on Snodgrass Hill. There, Thomas and his men held their ground despite repeated Confederate assaults. After dark, Thomas finally withdrew his exhausted and battle-weary troops for a nighttime retreat to Chattanooga.

The cost of Chickamauga was staggering. In one of the bloodiest battles of the war, the Confederates lost more than 18,000 men; Federal losses totaled nearly 16,000. The resounding defeat forced the Union army into Chattanooga, where, surrounded by Confederates occupying the heights above, the men faced possible starvation or surrender. But help came in October when General Joseph Hooker arrived with 20,000 reinforcements from Virginia. General William T. Sherman marched from Mississippi with 16,000 more in November. Relieved from its precarious position, the Union army prepared to plunge back into Georgia and attack the Confederate stronghold of Atlanta.

Kennesaw Mountain National Battlefield Park

Just three miles north of Marietta, Kennesaw Mountain rears boldly from the surrounding plain. More than 125 years ago, soldiers clad in blue and gray grappled in a deadly fight on the mountain's rugged, rocky slopes. Today, the scenes of the heaviest fighting have been preserved as Kennesaw Mountain National Battlefield Park, administered by the National Park Service.

In the spring of 1864, with Chattanooga and its vital railroad link finally secured, General William T. Sherman received bold new orders. He was to march into Georgia, crush the enemy army, and inflict as much damage as possible upon the South's war resources. When Sherman and his army, 100,000 strong, crossed into Georgia in early May, General Joseph E. Johnston and his 65,000 war-hardened Confederates were there to greet them.

The two armies quickly clashed, first at Resaca, then at New

Hope Church, Pickett's Mill, and Dallas. By skillfully outflanking his Southern opposition and threatening their railroad supply line, Sherman continually forced Johnston to fall back closer to Atlanta, the railroad hub of the South and major war manufacturing center for the Confederacy. By mid-June, Johnston had withdrawn to a formidable defensive line anchored at Kennesaw Mountain, barely 20 miles from the heart of the city. The time had come for yet another battle. In the humid heat of a southern summer, Sherman attacked.

The two-pronged assault was launched shortly after dawn on June 27. Astride Burnt Hickory Road, 5,500 Union soldiers lunged forward to capture the Confederate positions. But a deadly storm of lead and iron drove them back before reaching their goal, a mountain spur known today as Pigeon Hill. Watching the resulting bloodbath, Sherman quickly called off the attack.

The fiercest fighting of the battle took place at Cheatham Hill, present-day site of the Illinois Monument. Here, five brigades of Union infantry attempted to dislodge two Confederate divisions firmly entrenched atop the hill. Against staggering odds, Sherman's men stormed the defenders' earthworks. So aggressive was the assault, and so brutal the fighting, dead and wounded were heaped indiscriminately in the trenches. The assault wave soon melted under the blistering fire.

When the smoke cleared, Sherman had lost 3,000 men; Johnston 800. Although a Union defeat, the battle of Kennesaw Mountain proved a major stepping stone in the Atlanta campaign. Sherman immediately resumed his flanking maneuvers, forcing Johnston to again fall back, this time to his fortifications within Atlanta. Several battles and scarcely one month later, the city was evacuated.

The fall of Atlanta brought the bitter "fight to the finish" significantly closer to its end. In November, Sherman left Atlanta in ruins and began his devastating March to the Sea.

Pickett's Mill Battlefield

On May 27, 1864, Union and Confederate armies clashed in a brief but bloody battle at Pickett's Mill. In the thick woods surrounding a small gristmill just 27 miles from Atlanta, 14,000 Federal troops under Major General Oliver Howard attempted to dislodge 10,000 Confederates under General Patrick Cleburne. The result proved an embarrassing defeat for the Federals.

Around five o'clock in the afternoon, following a grueling five-hour march, Howard sent in Brigadier General William B.

Hazen with the first line of the Federal assault. Lacking time for a proper reconnaissance and hampered by dense foliage, Hazen's men soon blundered into a steep ravine in front of the Confederate defenses. There, they became easy prey for Confederate infantry commanded by Brigadier General Hiram S. Granbury. Despite the carnage fast occurring around them, Hazen's men desperately pushed forward, climbing to the top of the ravine and engaging Granbury's defenders at close range, in some places fighting hand-to-hand. But the unevenly matched contest was soon over. Exhausted from marching and crippled by passage through the ravine, Hazen's brigade was effectively destroyed in less than an hour.

Due to a mix-up in orders, the second wave of the Federal assault, led by Colonel William H. Gibson, did not follow upon the heels of Hazen's men as Howard had originally intended. When Gibson's brigade finally moved forward, 45 minutes late, Hazen's brigade had already been repulsed. Instead of reinforcing Hazen's assault, Gibson's troops found themselves alone, trapped in the same dangerous ravine, and exposed to the same withering fire of Granbury's men. Like Hazen, Gibson and his men were also repulsed in short order.

Howard had seen enough. In just a few hours of bitter fighting, the Federals had suffered a staggering loss of more than 1,600 killed and wounded, compared to less than 500 Confederate casualties. Howard entrenched his lines and called for reinforcements. Although occasional skirmishes occurred during the following week, the major fighting was over at Pickett's Mill. When the Confederates quietly withdrew to stronger fortifications closer to Atlanta, Howard's men rejoined General Sherman in the Federal conquest of that city.

Andersonville Prison

Officially known as Camp Sumter during the Civil War, Andersonville Prison was built by the Confederacy to house Union captives. Located ten miles northeast of Americus, the camp was designed to hold a maximum of 10,000 prisoners. But with increased military activity in Georgia, the stockade soon swelled with more than three times that number. Due to lack of supplies and severe overcrowding, Andersonville Prison quickly became a ghastly death camp where nearly 13,000 men perished in just 14 months.

In early 1864, a 16-acre clearing was cut deep in a pine forest near Anderson Station, on the rail line running from Macon to

Eufaula. A sturdy 15-foot-high stockade was erected, with sentry boxes perched along the top at 30-yard intervals. Herded into the stockade in February, prisoners found no shelter from the sun, wind, cold, or rain other than what they could crudely fashion from sticks, blankets, and other scarce materials. Quickly filled to capacity, the prison was enlarged to 26 acres in June, but prisoners continued pouring in at the rate of nearly 400 per day. By August, more than 32,000 sick and starving men were crowded into the camp.

The creek which provided most of the prisoners' drinking water was soon tainted with sewage from the latrines and refuse from the camp bakery. With the breakdown of the formal prisoner exchange system, the deficiency of resources in the South, and the war-wrecked Southern economy, the Confederacy could not provide adequate food, shelter, or medical supplies to its Federal captives. As a result, scurvy, diarrhea, and dysentery broke out in epidemic proportions.

So vile were the living conditions, between February 1864 and April 1865, 12,912 Union prisoners died from disease, malnutrition, and exposure. Their bodies were placed side by side in long trenches marked only with simple wooden posts in which numbers were carved. Private Dorance Atwater, a Federal prisoner placed in charge of the Death Register, secretly copied the list and smuggled it out in the lining of his coat when he was released in March of 1865. After the war, Clara Barton used Atwater's list to replace the wooden posts with headstones recording the prisoner's name, number, and home state. But even Atwater's extensive list proved incomplete: nearly 500 graves are simply marked "Unknown U.S. Soldier."

Andersonville Prison was closed on April 10, 1865, just one day after Lee surrendered to Grant at Appomattox. The prison keeper, Captain Henry Wirz, was arrested and tried for alleged war crimes by a special military commission. Though his guilt or innocence remains controversial to this day, Wirz was convicted and sentenced to death. He was executed in Washington, D.C. on November 10, 1865.

Today, nearly all traces of the old prison have faded into the Georgia landscape. Essentially all that remains are the ubiquitous rows of gravestones. Established on July 26, 1865, Andersonville National Historic Site permanently honors the final resting place for these ill-fated prisoners, and serves as a somber reminder of the many atrocities of war.

Double-Barrelled Cannon

The Civil War saw many innovative means of destruction brought to the battlefield. Among them was a novel, double-barrelled cannon cast at the Athens Foundry and Machine Works in 1862. Designed by John Gilleland, the unusual weapon was to simultaneously fire two cannonballs connected by an eight-foot iron chain. In theory, the balls were to pull the chain taut and sweep across open fields, mowing down hapless enemy soldiers. In practice, however, the barrels rarely fired at the same time. As a result, the chain inevitably broke and the balls spun harmlessly off in directions other than the one desired. After the war, the relic was placed on the lawn outside the Athens City Hall. There it remains, pointing north just in case.

Appendix
Site Locations and Visiting Hours

Chapter 1: Native Americans and Ancient Cultures

Etowah Mounds
    Etowah Mounds State Historic Site
    813 Indian Mounds Road SW
    Cartersville, GA 30120
    (706) 387-3747
    Located off GA 61, 5 miles southwest of I-75 at Cartersville.
    Visiting Hours: Tuesday - Saturday 9-5
                    Sunday 2-5:30
                    (Closed Mondays and major holidays)
    Admission: $1.50 adults/.75 children

Ocmulgee National Monument
    1207 Emery Highway
    Macon, GA 31201
    (912) 752-8257
    Located off US 80, east of I-16 near downtown Macon.
    Visiting Hours: Open daily 9-5
    Admission: Free

Kolomoki Mounds
    Kolomoki Mounds State Park
    Route 1, Box 114
    Blakely, GA 31723
    (912) 723-5296
    Located off US 27, 6 miles north of Blakely.
    Visiting Hours: Open daily from 7 a.m. to 10 p.m.
    Admission: $2.00 vehicle entry fee

Fort Mountain
   Fort Mountain State Park
   Route 7, Box 7008
   Chatsworth, GA 30705
   (706) 695-2621
   Located off GA 52, 7 miles east of Chatsworth.
   Visiting Hours: Open daily from 7 a.m. to 10 p.m.
   Admission: $2.00 vehicle entry fee

New Echota
   New Echota State Historic Site
   1211 Chatsworth Highway NE
   Calhoun, GA 30701
   (706) 629-8151
   Located off GA 225, 3 miles northeast of Calhoun.
   Visiting Hours: Tuesday - Saturday 9-5
                        Sunday 2-5:30
                        (Closed Mondays and major holidays)
   Admission: $1.50 adults/.75 children

Vann House
   Chief Vann House State Historic Site
   Route 7, Box 7655
   Chatsworth, GA 30705
   (706) 695-2598
   Located at intersection of GA 52 and GA 225, west of
   Chatsworth.
   Visiting Hours: Tuesday - Saturday 9-5
                        Sunday 2-5:30
                        (Closed Mondays and major holidays)
   Admission: $1.50 adults/.75 children

Rock Eagle Effigy Mound
    Located at the State 4-H Center, off US 441 between Eatonton
    and Madison.
    Visiting Hours: Open daily from sunrise to sunset
    Admission: Free

Chapter 2: Sentries by the Sea

Tybee Island Lighthouse
    Tybee Island Historical Society
    PO Box 366
    Tybee Island, GA 31328
    (912) 786-5801
    Located off US 80 on Tybee Island.
    Visiting Hours: April - September
                                  Open daily 10-6
                                  (Closed Tuesdays)
                           October - March
                                  Monday, Wednesday - Friday 12-4
                                  Saturday and Sunday 10-4
                                  (Closed Tuesdays)
    Admission: $2.50 adults/.75 children

St. Simons Lighthouse
    PO Box 1136
    St. Simons, GA 31522
    (912) 638-4666
    Located off Ocean Boulevard on St. Simons Island.
    Visiting Hours: Tuesday - Saturday 10-5
                           Sunday 1:30-5
                           (Closed Mondays and major holidays)
    Admission: $3.00 adults/$1.00 children

Sapelo Island Lighthouse
    c/o Darien Welcome Center
    PO Box 1497
    Darien, GA 31305
    (912) 437-6684
    Located on southern tip of Sapelo Island, accessible only by tour.
    Contact the Darien Welcome Center for information on tours to
    Sapelo Island.

Chapter 3: Timbered Tunnels Through Time

Watson Mill Covered Bridge
    Watson Mill Bridge State Park
    Route 1, Box 190
    Comer, GA 30629
    (706) 783-5349
    Located off GA 22, 5 miles south of Comer.
    Visiting Hours: Open daily 7 a.m. to 10 p.m.
    Admission: $2.00 vehicle entry fee

Red Oak Creek Covered Bridge
    Located off GA 85, on county road 4 miles north of Woodbury.
    Visiting Hours: Open daily from sunrise to sunset
    Admission: Free

Auchumpkee Creek Covered Bridge
    Located off US 19, on Allen Road 12 miles south of Thomaston.
    Visiting Hours: Open daily from sunrise to sunset
    Admission: Free

Pool's Mill Covered Bridge
   Located on Settendown Creek, 4 miles north of Ducktown and
   GA 20.
   Visiting Hours: Open daily from sunrise to sunset
   Admission: Free

Coheelee Creek Covered Bridge
   Located on Old River Road at Coheelee Creek, 2 miles north of
   Hilton.
   Visiting Hours: Open daily from sunrise to sunset
   Admission: Free

Lowry Covered Bridge
   Located on Euharlee Creek off GA 113 west of Cartersville.
   Visiting Hours: Open daily from sunrise to sunset
   Admission: Free

Stone Mountain Covered Bridge
   Stone Mountain Memorial Park
   Box 778
   Stone Mountain, GA 30086
   (404) 498-5600
   Located off US 78, 15 miles east of Atlanta.
   Visiting Hours: Grounds open daily from 6 a.m. to midnight
   Admission: $5.00 vehicle entry fee

Chapter 4: Grist for the Mill

Hamburg Mill
  Hamburg Mill State Park
  Route 1, Box 233
  Mitchell, GA 30820
  (912) 552-2393
  Located off GA 102, 6 miles northeast of Warthen via Hamburg
  Road.
  Visiting Hours: Open daily from 7 a.m. to 10 p.m.
  Admission: $2.00 vehicle entry fee

Watson Mill
  George L. Smith State Park
  PO Box 57
  Twin City, GA 30471
  (912) 763-2759
  Located off GA 23, 4 miles southeast of Twin City.
  Visiting Hours: Open daily from 7 a.m. to 10 p.m.
  Admission: $2.00 vehicle entry fee

Cochran Mills
  (404) 463-6304
  Location: This is one of the more difficult sites to find, but
worth the effort. Traveling south on US 29 out of Fairburn, Georgia,
turn right on Wilkerson Mill Road just past the Cessna airport.
Follow Wilkerson Mill Road for 4 miles until it dead-ends on
Cochran Mill Road. Turn right and go 1 mile to Cochran Mill Park.
The ruins are to the right of Cochran Mill Road, down a gravel path
which is closed to vehicular traffic.
  Visiting Hours: Open daily from sunrise to sunset
  Admission: Free

151

Prater's Mill
101 Timberline Drive
Dalton, GA 30721
Located off GA 2, 1 mile west of GA 71, 10 miles north of
Dalton.
Visiting Hours: Grounds are open daily from sunrise to sunset
(Mill is open only during special events)
Admission: Free except during special events

Berry College's Old Mill
Berry College
2277 Martha Berry Boulevard
Mt. Berry Station
Rome, GA 30149
(706) 232-5374
Located off US 27, 1 mile north of Rome.
Visiting Hours: Open daily from sunrise to sunset
Admission: Free

Chapter 5: Early Industry and Trade

Columbus Iron Works
801 Front Street
Columbus, GA 31902
(706) 322-1613
Located on Front Street in downtown Columbus.
Visiting Hours: Open Monday - Saturday 9-5
Admission: Free

Confederate Powder Works
Located on Augusta Canal near downtown Augusta.
Visiting Hours: Open daily sunrise to sunset
Admission: Free

Cooper Iron Works
(706) 382-4700
Located just downstream from the Allatoona Dam on the Etowah
River.
Visiting Hours: Summer: Open daily 8 a.m. to 10 p.m.
                    Winter: Open daily 8 a.m. to sunset
Admission: Free

Central of Georgia Railway Roundhouse
601 West Harris
Savannah, GA 31402
(912) 651-6823
Located on West Harris Street near downtown Savannah.
Visiting Hours: Monday - Saturday 10-4
                    Sunday 12-4
Admission: $2.50 adults/$2.00 children

Augusta Cotton Exchange
32 Eighth Street at Riverwalk
Augusta, GA 30901
(706) 724-4067
Located on Eighth Street in downtown Augusta.
Visiting Hours: Monday - Saturday 9-5
                    Sunday 1-5
Admission: Free

Butler Island Plantation
    Located off US 17, 1 mile south of bridge at Darien.
    Visiting Hours: Open daily from sunrise to sunset
    Admission: Free

McIntosh Sugar Works
    Located at intersection of GA Spur 40 and Kings Bay Road, near
    entrance to the Kings Bay Naval Submarine Base.
    Visiting Hours: Open daily from sunrise to sunset
    Admission: Free

Chapter 6: The Best Dam Sites in Georgia

High Falls Dam
    High Falls State Park
    Route 5, Box 202-A
    Jackson, GA 30233
    (912) 994-5080
    Located off I-75, 10 miles north of Forsyth.
    Visiting Hours: Open daily from 7 a.m. to 10 p.m.
    Admission: $2.00 vehicle entry fee

Morgan Falls Hydroelectric Power Plant
    Located off Morgan Falls Road on the Chattahoochee River
    north of Atlanta.
    Visiting Hours: Open daily from sunrise to sunset
    Admission: Free

Lloyd Shoals Hydroelectric Plant
   Located on the Ocmulgee River, north of GA 16 between Butts
   and Jasper counties.
   Visiting Hours: Open daily from sunrise to sunset
   Admission: Free

Tallulah Falls Dam
   Terrora Park Visitor Center
   Highway 23/441
   PO Box 9
   Tallulah Falls, GA 30573
   (706) 754-3276
   Located off US 441, 1/2 mile north of Tallulah Falls.
   Visiting Hours: Open daily from sunrise to sunset
   Admission: Free

Tugalo Dam
   Terrora Park Visitor Center
   Highway 23/441
   PO Box 9
   Tallulah Falls, GA 30573
   (706) 754-3276
   Located off US 441, 1 mile south of Tallulah Falls.
   Visiting Hours: Open daily from sunrise to sunset
   Admission: Free

Chapter 7: Georgia Potpourri

Sweetwater Creek Ruins
Sweetwater Creek State Park
PO Box 816
Lithia Springs, GA 30057
(404) 944-1700
Located off I-20, 15 miles west of Atlanta.
Visiting Hours: Open daily from 8 a.m. to sunset
Admission: $2.00 vehicle entry fee

Scull Shoals Ruins
Located on east bank of Oconee River off GA 15, 12 miles north of Greensboro.
Visiting Hours: Open daily from sunrise to sunset
Admission: Free

Sope Creek Ruins
Chattahoochee River National Recreation Area
1978 Island Ford Parkway
Dunwoody, GA 30340
(404) 394-8835
Located on Paper Mill Road in Sope Creek unit of the Chattahoochee River National Recreation Area.
Visiting Hours: Open daily from sunrise to sunset
Admission: Free

Sunbury
> Route 1, Box 236
> Midway, GA 31320
> (912) 884-5999
> Located 8 miles east of I-95 (Exit #13) via GA 38.
> Visiting Hours: Open daily from sunrise to sunset
> Admission: Free

Christ Church
> PO Box 1185
> St. Simons Island, GA 31522
> (912) 638-8683
> Located on St. Simons Island.
> Visiting Hours: Summer: Open daily 2-5
>   Winter: Open daily 1-4
> Admission: Free (donations accepted)

Dahlonega Gold Museum
> Public Square, Box 2042
> Dahlonega, GA 30533
> (706) 864-2257
> Located on the Public Square in Dahlonega.
> Visiting Hours: Monday - Saturday 9-5
>   Sunday 10-5
> Admission: $1.50 adults/.75 children

Stone Mountain's Confederate Memorial Carving
    Stone Mountain Memorial Park
    Box 778
    Stone Mountain, GA 30086
    (404) 498-5600
    Located off US 78, 15 miles east of Atlanta.
    Visiting Hours: Grounds open daily from 6 a.m. to midnight
    Admission: $5.00 vehicle entry fee

Porterdale Mills
    Located off I-20, 4 miles southwest of Covington.
    Visiting Hours: Grounds open daily from sunrise to sunset
    Admission: Free

Chapter 8: There's No Place Like Home

Little White House
    Little White House State Historic Site
    Route 1, Box 10
    Warm Springs, GA 31830
    (706) 655-3511
    Located off GA 85W, 1/2 mile south of Warm Springs.
    Visiting Hours: Open daily 9-5
                        (Closed major holidays)
    Admission: $3.00 adults/$1.50 children

Liberty Hall
   Alexander Stephens State Historic Site
   PO Box 235
   Crawfordville, GA 30631
   (706) 456-2602
   Located within the city limits of Crawfordville.
   Visiting Hours: Tuesday - Saturday 9-5
                       Sunday 2-5:30
                       (Closed Mondays and major holidays)
   Admission: $1.50 adults/.75 children

Oak Hill
   Berry College
   2277 Martha Berry Boulevard
   Mt. Berry Station
   Rome, GA 30149
   (706) 232-5374
   Located off US 27, 1 mile north of Rome.
   Visiting Hours: Tuesday - Saturday 10-5
                       Sunday 1-5
                       (Closed Mondays and holidays)
   Admission: $3.00 adults/$1.50 children

Wormslow
   Wormslow State Historic Site
   7601 Skidaway Road
   Savannah, GA 31406
   (912) 353-3023
   Located on Skidaway Road, 8 miles southeast of downtown
   Savannah.
   Visiting Hours: Tuesday - Saturday 9-5
                       Sunday 2-5:30
                       (Closed Mondays and major holidays)
   Admission: $1.50 adults/.75 children

Horton House
    Located along North Riverview Drive on Jekyll Island.
    Visiting Hours: Open daily from sunrise to sunset
    Admission: Free

Jarrell Plantation
    Jarrell Plantation State Historic Site
    Route 2, Box 220
    Juliette, GA 31046
    (912) 986-5172
    Located off US 23, 15 miles north of Macon.
    Visiting Hours: Tuesday - Saturday 9-5
                       Sunday 2-5:30
                       (Closed Mondays and major holidays)
    Admission: $1.50 adults/.75 children

Hay House
    934 Georgia Avenue
    Macon, GA 31201
    (912) 742-8155
    Located on Georgia Avenue in downtown Macon.
    Visiting Hours: Monday - Saturday 10-5
                       Sunday 1-5
                       (Closed holidays)
    Admission: $4.00 adults/$2.00 children

Rhodes Hall
    1516 Peachtree Street, NW
    Atlanta, GA 30309
    (404) 881-9980
    Located on Peachtree Street in downtown Atlanta.
    Visiting Hours: Open Monday - Friday 11-4
    Admission: $2.00 adults/.50 children

Herndon Home
    587 University Place NW
    Atlanta, GA 30314
    (404) 581-9813
    Located near Atlanta University in downtown Atlanta.
    Visiting Hours: Open Tuesday - Saturday 10-4
        (Closed Sundays, Mondays, and holidays)
    Admission: Free

Travelers Rest
    Travelers Rest State Historic Site
    Route 3
    Toccoa, GA 30577
    (706) 886-2256
    Located 6 miles northeast of Toccoa on US 123.
    Visiting Hours: Tuesday - Saturday 9-5
        Sunday 2-5:30
        (Closed Mondays and major holidays)
    Admission: $1.50 adults/.75 children

Chapter 9: In Defense of the Land

Fort King George
    Fort King George State Historic Site
    PO Box 711
    Darien, GA 31305
    (912) 437-4770
    Located in Darien, 3 miles east of I-95.
    Visiting Hours: Tuesday - Saturday 9-5
                     Sunday 2-5:30
                     (Closed Mondays and major holidays)
    Admission: $1.50 adults/.75 children

Fort Frederica National Monument
    Route 9, Box 286-C
    St. Simons, GA 31522
    (912) 638-3639
    Located on St. Simons Island.
    Visiting Hours: Open daily 8-5
    Admission: $2.00 adults/children free

Fort Morris
    Fort Morris State Historic Site
    Route 1, Box 236
    Midway, GA 31320
    (912) 884-5999
    Located 7 miles east of I-95 (Exit #13) via GA 38.
    Visiting Hours: Tuesday - Saturday 9-5
                     Sunday 2-5:30
                     (Closed Mondays and major holidays)
    Admission: $1.50 adults/.75 children

Fort Jackson
    1 Fort Jackson Road
    Savannah, GA 31404
    (912) 232-3945
    Located on US 80, 3 miles east of Savannah.
    Visiting Hours: Open daily 9-5
                        (Closed major holidays)
    Admission: $2.50 adults/$2.00 children

Fort McAllister
    Fort McAllister State Historic Site
    PO Box 394-A
    Richmond Hill, GA 31324
    (912) 727-2339
    Located 10 miles east of I-95 (Exit #15), off GA Spur 144.
    Visiting Hours: Tuesday - Saturday 9-5
                        Sunday 2-5:30
                        (Closed Mondays and major holidays)
    Admission: $1.50 adults/.75 children

Fort Pulaski National Monument
    PO Box 30757
    Savannah, GA 31410
    (912) 786-5787
    Located off US 80, on Cockspur Island east of Savannah.
    Visiting Hours: Open daily from 8:30-5:30
    Admission: $2.00 adults/children free

Fort Yargo
   PO Box 764
   Winder, GA 30680
   (404) 867-3489
   Located off GA 81, 1 mile south of Winder.
   Visiting Hours: Open daily from 7 a.m. to 10 p.m.
   Admission: $2.00 vehicle entry fee

Chapter 10: Lest We Forget

Chickamauga Battlefield
   PO Box 2128
   Fort Oglethorpe, GA 30742
   (706) 866-9241
   Located on US 27, 2 miles south of Fort Oglethorpe.
   Visiting Hours: Open daily from sunrise to sunset
   Admission: Free

Kennesaw Mountain National Battlefield Park
   900 Kennesaw Mountain Drive
   Kennesaw, GA 30144-4854
   (404) 427-4686
   Located 3 miles north of Marietta.
   Visiting Hours: Open daily 8:30-5
   Admission: Free

Pickett's Mill Battlefield
  Pickett's Mill Battlefield State Historic Site
  2640 Mt. Tabor Road
  Dallas, GA 30132
  (404) 443-7850
  Located off GA 381, 5 miles northeast of Dallas.
  Visiting Hours: Tuesday - Saturday 9-5
                      Sunday 2-5:30
                      (Closed Mondays and major holidays)
  Admission: $1.50 adults/.75 children

Andersonville Prison
  Andersonville National Historic Site
  Route 1, Box 85
  Andersonville, GA 31711
  (912) 924-0343
  Located off GA 49, 10 miles northeast of Americus.
  Visiting Hours: Open daily 8-5
  Admission: Free

Double-Barrelled Cannon
  Located outside the city hall in Athens.
  Visiting Hours: Open daily from sunrise to sunset
  Admission: Free

Index

169

Site Suggestion for *Georgia Snapshots*

Site Name: _____

Location: _____

_____

Description: _____

_____

Historical Significance: _____

_____

_____

Your Name: _____

Address: _____

_____

_____

Mail to: *Georgia Snapshots*
Adele Enterprises
PO Box 553
Union City, GA 30291-0553

Thank you for your suggestion!

Order Form

Please send __ copies of *Georgia Snapshots: Glances at the Past*. I have enclosed a check or money order for $12.95 per book, plus a $2.00 shipping charge.

Name: _____

Address: _____

City: _____

State: _____ Zip Code: _____

Mail to: *Georgia Snapshots*
Adele Enterprises
PO Box 553
Union City, GA 30291-0553

Thank you for your order!